Kids on Strike!

KIDS ON STRIKE!

Susan Campbell Bartoletti

HOUGHTON MIFFLIN COMPANY

BOSTON

For my daughter, Brandy, with love

The text of this book is set in Monotype Bulmer.

Book design and maps by Lisa Diercks

Photos pp. i–ii: Library of Congress

Photo p. 196: Photography Collection, University of Maryland Baltimore County

Library of Congress Cataloging-in-Publication Data

Bartoletti, Susan Campbell.

Kids on strike! / by Susan Campbell Bartoletti.

p.   cm.

Summary: Describes the conditions and treatment that drove working children to strike, from the mill
workers' strike in 1834 and the coal strikes at the turn of the century to the children who marched with
Mother Jones in 1903.

ISBN 0-395-88892-1

1. Strikes and lockouts — United States — History — Juvenile literature. 2. Children — Employment
— United States — History — Juvenile literature. [1. Strikes and lockouts — History. 2. Children —
Employment — History.]   I. Title.

HD5324.B37   1999   98-50575

331.892'973 — dc21   CIP   AC

Manufactured in the United States of America

KPT 10 9 8 7 6 5 4 3

Acknowledgments

I could not have completed this book without the help and support of the following people and institutions: Thomas Dublin and Liz Rosenberg, faculty members at Binghamton University, the State University of New York; Chester Kulesa, Scranton Anthracite Heritage Museum; Mark Bograd, Lowell National Historic Park; Ken Skulski, Immigrant City Archives; Betsy Moylan, librarian extraordinaire, University of Scranton; John Beck and Tim Ford, University of Maryland, Baltimore County; Charles Kumpas; librarians at the Library of Congress, the Kheel Center at Cornell University, Binghamton University; Dominic Keating; Elisabeth Burger, daughter of Pauline Newman's best friend; Tom Harrison, grandson of Gus Rangnow; Karen Klockner and Kim Keller, editors and friends; Barrie Van Dyck, agent and friend; and my husband and children, Joe, Brandy, and Joey, who put up with research vacations.

Contents

"SHALL WE TURN OUT?"

Harriet Hanson and the Spinning-Room Strikers

The rows of spinning machines whirred and whizzed around ten-year-old Harriet Hanson. She watched as the cotton threads were drawn out, twisted tightly into yarn, and wound around the whirling bobbins.

"I can see myself now," Harriet wrote years later in her autobiography, "racing down the alley, between the spinning-frames, carrying in front of me a bobbin-box bigger than I was."

Like most of the youngest mill workers, Harriet was a bobbin girl, or "doffer." When the wooden bobbins were full, her job was to

This young mill girl is bending over cylinders of cotton roving. The cylinders are delivered to the spinning room, where the roving is drawn out and wound onto smaller bobbins. Lowell National Historical Park

"doff," or "do off," the full bobbins of yarn and replace them with empty ones. Doffers had to work fast, so that the spinning frames weren't stopped for too long.

"I Wanted to Earn Money"

Harriet Hanson lived with her widowed mother and three brothers and sisters in Lowell, Massachusetts, the first textile factory town in the United States.

Harriet's father had died in 1831, when she was six, and her mother found it difficult to earn enough money to support a family.

Mrs. Hanson found a job as matron of a factory-owned boardinghouse, and, for a few years, young Harriet attended school regularly and helped her mother. "My mother kept forty boarders, most of them men, mill-hands," wrote Harriet. "My part in the housework was to wash the dishes, and I was obliged to stand on a cricket [a low wooden stool] in order to reach the sink."

In 1835, when Harriet turned ten, she asked her mother if she could work in a nearby cotton mill. "I wanted to earn money like the other little girls," she recalled. Mrs. Hanson gave her consent.

Harriet was assigned as a doffer in the spinning workroom. Each day, she rose at four-thirty in the morning and washed quickly, using a pitcher of water and basin in her room. She tied up her hair and followed the older mill girls to work, down the street and across the canal.

Work began promptly at five o'clock. Harriet and the other mill girls worked fourteen hours each weekday and eight hours on Saturdays. They had brief breaks for breakfast and dinner and were given only three unpaid holidays each year: Fast Day in the spring, the Fourth of July, and Thanksgiving. They worked fewer hours during the winter, when there was not as much daylight.

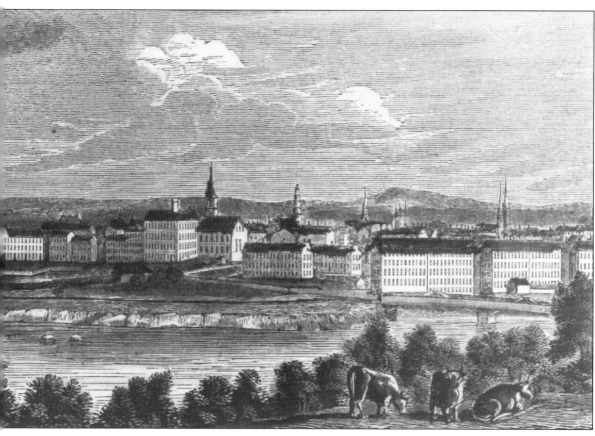

Lowell, Massachusetts, was the first large-scale, planned industrial city in the United States. For many years, it was considered a model factory town.
Lowell Historical Society

At work Harriet watched the older mill girls tend the spinning machines. The girls kept a close eye on the cotton thread. When a thread broke, the spinner quickly pieced the ends together.

After the wooden bobbins were filled, they were delivered to the weaving room, where the finished cloth was made. Older girls and young women tended the weaving looms, making sure each bobbin was full of thread. When a bobbin was empty, the girl stopped the loom, inserted a new bobbin, re-threaded the shuttle, then started the loom again. Like the spinners, the weavers also watched for broken threads.

Mill girls began work promptly at five o'clock each morning. Winslow Homer showed the mill girls walking to the factory in time for the morning bell.
Lowell National Historical Park

By the end of each long workday, the mill girls were exhausted. They suffered from ringing ears, backaches, sore legs, and swollen feet. Young doffers like Harriet were tired, too, even though it took only fifteen minutes out of every hour to change the bobbins. "The doffers were forced to be on duty fourteen hours a day," Harriet wrote. "It has taken nearly a lifetime for me to make up the sleep lost at that early age."

"A Pleasant Life"
Throughout the 1830s and 1840s, most of the New England mill girls were young teenage girls or unmarried women between the ages of fifteen and twenty-five. Often the daughters of Yankee farmers, they moved from surrounding farms and villages to factory towns like Lowell. Most lived in

Winslow Homer depicted a woman winding shuttle bobbins. Her hair was tied back so it wouldn't get caught in the machinery. Lowell National Historical Park

The long row of brick boardinghouses are close to the mill, located at the end of the street. Lowell National Historical Park

boardinghouses that were owned by the factory corporations and run by matrons like Harriet's mother. The rest lived with their parents or other relatives in Lowell.

Thirty to forty girls lived in one boardinghouse. Four to six girls slept in one small bedroom, two girls to a bed. The bedrooms were crowded with the girls' belongings. Each girl usually brought a homemade bandbox, a round cardboard container that held small articles of clothing. She also owned a work dress, a Sunday dress, a shawl, one or two aprons, books, papers, writing materials, and a few treats such as candy or sweet breads. A spare bedroom served as an infirmary. The girls ate their suppers in a large communal dining room.

Boardinghouse regulations were strict: the girls had to agree to work for at least twelve months in the mill, give two weeks' notice before quitting, attend church regularly, follow curfews, and demonstrate good moral character. Otherwise, girls were fired and "blacklisted." If a girl's name appeared on the blacklist, she was prevented from obtaining a job in any other mill.

Despite the restrictions, Harriet noted, "It was a pleasant life." The mill girls formed close bonds and even began "improvement circles" so that they could study literature, science, and religion. They kept diaries and journals. The older girls taught the younger girls and told them stories. In the evenings and on Sundays, the girls read books from the circulating libraries and attended lectures, plays, horticultural shows, and concerts. Eager to dress in the latest styles, they enjoyed shopping, and they bought new dresses, shoes, shawls, and hats. They happily discarded their farm clothes.

Many mill girls were excited about their new opportunities. For most, it was the first time their labor was considered important enough to earn money. Some sent money home to help pay farm mortgages, send brothers to college, or support widowed mothers. Some also saved their money to pay for their own education, dowries, or to buy things for themselves.

Harriet, like many others, took pride in her work and her wages. She wrote: "How proud I was when my turn came to stand up on the bobbin-box, and write my name in the paymaster's book."

"Naturally I Took Sides"

When the mills first opened, the girls seemed contented. The factory owners and investors were also contented with the mills' huge profits.

As time went on, more mills were built throughout New England. Soon economic conditions changed as the competing textile mills produced more and more cloth. In order to sell the cloth, the mill owners lowered the prices, which reduced their profits.

Although the mill owners continued to prosper, they missed their huge

Each night, dinner was served in a large dining room on the first floor. Girls complained that they had to gulp down meals to get to work on time.
Lowell National Historical Park: Joseph Bartoletti

Four to six mill girls shared a crowded bedroom. The curfew bell rang at ten o'clock.
Lowell National Historical Park: Joseph Bartoletti

profits. They sought ways to make more money. They forced the girls to speed up their work and to tend as many as three or four looms. Bonuses were paid to overseers whose workers turned out the greatest amount of product. Some overseers forced the girls to work on empty stomachs because they thought the girls would work harder.

For many girls, it was no longer a pleasant life. In 1834, when the mill owners announced a cut in wages, the mill girls organized. They gave two weeks' quitting notice and withdrew their savings from the banks. The mill owners fired one of the strike ringleaders. As she left the mill office, she waved her hat as a signal. Eight hundred mill girls "turned out" in response.

During the short strike, the girls had little support. In Sunday sermons, ministers preached that the girls should return to work and be grateful for their jobs. Newspapers also criticized the strikers. The mill owners advertised for replacement workers. After a few days, the girls gave in and returned to work at reduced wages. The strike leaders were fired.

The mill girls knew they had to stick together in order to defend their rights. They organized the Factory Girls' Association. Within two years, the association grew to 2,500 members.

In 1836, one year after Harriet Hanson began work at the mill, conditions worsened once again when the factory owners raised the cost of living at the boardinghouse with no increase in wages. The room and board hike amounted to a twelve and a half percent reduction in the girls' pay.

The mill girls were outraged. They elected leaders to speak to the factory owners. When the owners refused to negotiate, the girls planned a strike. "I worked in a lower room," said Harriet, "where I heard the proposed strike fully. . . . Naturally I took sides with the strikers."

The prospect of a strike frightened many workers. Would they lose their jobs? How would they survive without any money? What would happen to their families who depended on their wages? How could mere mill girls fight powerful factory owners? How would it look for girls to protest?

To others, the prospect sounded exciting. Their work and wages had

Hundreds of looms clanked and clanged in the weaving room for ten to fourteen hours a day. When the looms' movements became synchronized, the entire mill trembled. Lowell National Historical Park: Paul Dunigan

given them confidence and a sense of independence. They were the daughters of free men. Like their Yankee grandmothers and grandfathers, they were prepared to defend their rights. The girls assured the other workers that they *could* stand up to their powerful employers. One worker's voice was not strong enough, but an association of workers would be powerful indeed.

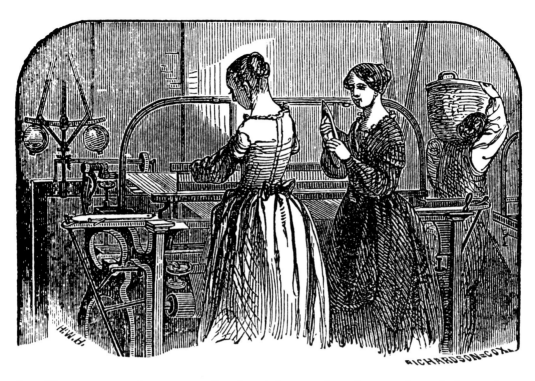

As mill owners sought more profit, the girls were forced to speed up their work and tend three or four looms. Lowell National Historical Park

"Shall We Turn Out?"

When the day of the strike arrived, the older girls and women who worked in the upper rooms of the mill turned out first. The spinners who worked in Harriet's room hesitated. They saw the strikers, but they were scared. No one wanted to be the first. Finally, eleven-year-old Harriet made up her mind. "I don't care what you do," she said. "I am going to turn out, whether any one else does or not." And she marched out the door.

Once outside in the mill yard, Harriet became aware of the spinners behind her. "As I looked back at the long line that followed me," Harriet wrote later in her autobiography, "I was more proud than I have ever been since at any success I may have achieved."

CHAPTER ONE

"A DEVIL IN PETTICOATS"

Young Mill Workers Rebel
Lowell, Massachusetts (1836)

Eleven-year-old Harriet Hanson and nearly two thousand other mill girls turned out during the 1836 Lowell strike—nearly one-third of the work force. The Factory Girls' Association coordinated strike activities, electing leaders and creating committees to raise funds for girls who couldn't afford room and board while they were on strike.

The strikers gave speeches and discussed their demands during open-air meetings. They announced that they would rather "die in the poorhouse than give in to the factory owners." They marched

These workers have gathered in the Boott Mills courtyard. Lowell Museum

through the streets, singing songs to raise their spirits and morale. They wrote their own words to popular tunes.

By the end of the month, the strikers ran out of money. The factory owners fought back by evicting the girls from the boardinghouses.

Because the factory owned nearly all the available housing, the girls had no place to stay. The factory owners also fired the strike leaders for "mutiny" and blacklisted them.

Harriet and her mother were in trouble, too. A factory agent visited Mrs. Hanson and scolded her for not being able to control her own daughter. "You could not prevent the older mill girls from turning out," he told Mrs. Hanson, "but your daughter is a child, and *her* you could control." He dismissed Mrs. Hanson from her position as a boardinghouse matron. Harriet and many other mill girls returned to work at reduced wages. Others quit their jobs and returned home.

To some, it may have appeared that the strike had failed, but the factory owners lost many of their experienced workers. Without those workers, the mills couldn't produce as much cloth as before the strike. For several months, the mills ran below capacity.

Yet the Lowell mill girls had accomplished something more. Many factory owners and foremen thought that young workers—especially girls—would accept whatever conditions were given to them. Children, they thought, would be less likely to protest than adults.

But the owners were wrong. Throughout the labor history of the United States, wherever children have worked, they have sought ways to improve their working and living conditions. One of the first children's strikes on record occurred in July 1828 in Paterson, New Jersey. When the Paterson cotton mill owners changed the noon dinner hour to one o'clock, the children quickly organized a strike. They wanted their noon dinner hour restored and their work day reduced from thirteen and a half hours to ten. After three weeks, the strike ended. The mill owners restored the dinner hour, but the work day remained the same. The strike leaders were fired.

Although not all working children protested, many did. They organized and helped one another. They negotiated. And when negotiations failed, they went on strike.

Thirty to forty mill girls lived in one boardinghouse. They formed close bonds and lasting friendships. Lowell National Historical Park

"I Thought It Would Be a Pleasure"

Children have always worked in the United States. They labored on farms, in fields, at home, and in shops. They worked as farmhands, domestic servants, and apprentices.

From the very first spinning mill built by Samuel Slater in 1790, children have been an important and cheap source of labor because owners didn't pay children as much as adults. Slater's first labor force consisted of seven boys and two girls between the ages of seven and twelve.

Many adults thought that children developed good moral training from

In the town of Lowell, the girls shopped, attended lectures and the theater, and read books from the circulating library. Lowell Historical Society

work and learned valuable lessons in thrift and economy. The factory and mill owners claimed that the industries would go bankrupt if children didn't work. They also said that families and society would suffer from an increase in "crime, wickedness, and pauperism."

Children also worked because their parents needed their wages. Parents used the money to buy food or pay rent and medical bills. Many children were eager to work, especially if they thought it would help their families. "I thought it would be a pleasure to feel I was not a trouble or a burden or expense to anybody," said Lucy Larcom, who worked in a Lowell mill when she was eleven.

Lucy longed to go to school, but she couldn't. "The little money I could earn—one dollar a week, besides the price of my board—was needed in my family."

Many New England mill girls welcomed the opportunity to work because it freed them from farm life, rural villages, and parental control and restrictions. Eager to experience life in a busy factory town, many girls begged their parents to allow them to work.

Some girls liked their independence so much that they complained if their families asked them to come home. A mill worker named Lucy Ann had hoped to work to save enough money to attend Oberlin College, but her father wanted her to return home. Lucy wrote a letter to her cousin, complaining bitterly about her father: "I have earned enough to school me awhile, and have not I a right to do so, or must I go home, like a dutiful girl, place the money in father's hands, and then there goes all my hard earnings. . . . Others may find fault with me, and call me selfish, but I think I should spend my earnings as I please."

During this time, women had few rights. They weren't allowed to vote. Married women could not own property in their own name or keep the money they earned. Women were expected to hand their wages over to their husbands. "A woman was not supposed to be capable of spending her own money," noted Harriet Hanson.

Some mill girls and women worked to support themselves after they ran away from abusive fathers or husbands. When visitors came to the mills, the runaways ducked and hid. "The laws said a husband could claim his wife wherever he found her, and also the children she was trying to shield from his influence," wrote Harriet. "I have seen more than one poor woman skulk behind her loom or her frame when visitors approached."

The laws were the same for young children, who could not keep the money they had earned, either. They turned their pay envelopes over to their parents, who used the money for necessities. Sometimes the parents gave the working children a few cents to spend.

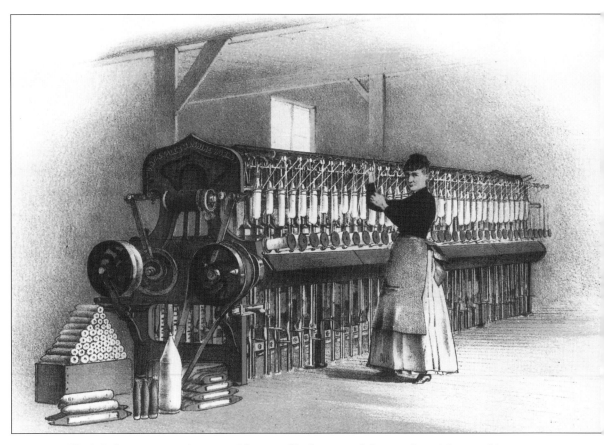

Many mill girls began as spinners. They walked up and down the aisle, tending the spinning frame. They watched as the cotton threads were drawn out and twisted then wound around bobbins. University of Massachusetts Lowell

"A Fiendish Spite"

Although some laborers initially found pleasure in working, the enjoyment faded quickly. There was so much to learn! New girls were assigned as "spare hands" to experienced workers. Spare hands weren't paid. It could take two or three months before a new worker was allowed to work by herself. Weavers had to manage two looms, and spinners had to tend one side of 128 spindles before they were assigned their own machinery.

To some girls, the machinery seemed monstrous. Lucy Larcom described the dressing frame that she tended: "[It] was as unmanageable as an overgrown child. It had to be watched in a dozen directions every minute and even then it was always getting itself and me into trouble. . . . The half-live creature, with its great groaning joints and whizzing fan was aware of my incapacity to manage it, and had a fiendish spite against me."

A fiendish spite indeed. In the weaving room, the carriage wheel rotated at a speed of seventy-five miles per hour. The leather belt on the carriage wheel weighed nine hundred pounds. The shuttles flew across the narrow wooden races at ninety miles per hour. One mishap from a carriage wheel, leather belt, or shuttle could seriously injure, maim, or kill a worker—especially a child.

But employers found the children's small bodies and the tiny

75 Young Women
From 15 to 35 Years of Age,
WANTED TO WORK IN THE
COTTON MILLS!
IN LOWELL AND CHICOPEE, MASS.

I am authorized by the Agents of said Mills to make the following proposition to persons suitable for their work, viz:—They will be paid $1.00 per week, and board, for the first month. It is presumed they will then be able to go to work at job prices. They will be considered as engaged for one year, cases of sickness excepted. I will pay the expenses of those who have not the means to pay for themselves, and the girls will pay it to the Company by their first labor. All that remain in the employ of the Company eighteen months will have the amount of their expenses to the Mills refunded to them. They will be properly cared for in sickness. It is hoped that none will go except those whose circumstances will admit of their staying at least one year. None but active and healthy girls will be engaged for this work, as it would not be advisable for either the girls or the Company.

I shall be at the Howard Hotel, Burlington, on Monday, July 25th; at Farnham's, St Albans, Tuesday forenoon, 26th, at Keyes's, Swanton, in the afternoon; at the Massachusetts' House, Rouses Point, on Wednesday, the 27th, to engage girls,—such as would like a place in the Mills would do well to improve the present opportunity, as new hands will not be wanted late in the season. I shall start with my Company, for the Mills, on Friday morning, the 29th inst., from Rouses Point, at 6 o'clock. Such as do not have an opportunity to see me at the above places, can take the cars and go with me the same as though I had engaged them.

I will be responsible for the safety of all baggage that is marked in care of I. M. BOYNTON, and delivered to my charge.

I. M. BOYNTON,
Agent for Procuring Help for the Mills.

Advertisements enticed young women to move to factory towns like Lowell. The girls usually worked for several years, then returned home or married. Some mill girls went on to school.
Baker Library, Graduate School of Business Administration, Harvard University

hands and fingers just the right size to clean and work the machinery. Eleven-year-old Al Priddy, who worked in a Bedford, Massachusetts, cotton mill, explained how he cleaned the spinning mules, the machines that spun the cotton fibers into yarn. "I had to clean fallers, which, like teeth, chopped down on one's hand, unless great speed and precautions were used," he said.

One day the carriage wheel cut off the end of Al Priddy's pinky finger. "But that was nothing at all compared to what happened to some of my friends," said Al. When one friend became pinned between the mule and iron post, his body was badly crushed. Another friend lost two fingers, and still another broke his back.

The machines weren't the only dangers. Over time, the tremendous noise caused hearing damage. Cotton lint swirled in the air, settling like snow on the floor, the machinery, and the children. "I breathed it down my nostrils," said Al Priddy. "It worked into my hair and was gulped down my throat." The lint made the children's lungs susceptible to tuberculosis and other diseases.

In order to keep the cotton threads from snapping, steam was sprayed into the air, and the windows were nailed shut to maintain the proper moisture. Temperatures ranged between 90 and 115 degrees Fahrenheit in the unventilated rooms. The hot, sticky, stuffy environment contributed to the spread of disease.

"A Devil in Petticoats"

In an effort to control the labor force, factory owners imposed strict rules. New England mill girls, for example, could be fired for immoral conduct, drinking, smoking, failure to attend church or comply with boardinghouse regulations, lying, suspicious character, unauthorized absence, laughing, hysteria, impudence, complaining about wages or the boss. Some girls were dismissed

simply because the overseer didn't like them. When a worker was fired, the boss wrote the reason beside her name. In one New Hampshire mill, a girl broke so many rules that she was called "a devil in petticoats."

Al Priddy considered the regulations worse than prison rules and the factory bosses more stern than prison guards. "There was a rule against looking out of a window," said Al. "There was a rule against reading during work hours. There was a rule preventing us from talking to one another. There was a rule prohibiting us from leaving the mill during work hours. We were not supposed to sit down, even though we had caught up with our work. We were never supposed to stop work, even when we could. There was a rule that anyone coming to work a minute late would lose his work."

When workers quit, the counting-room clerk signed them out. Beside each name, the clerk made notations in his leather-bound book. He indicated the kind of employee the worker had been. He noted whether the worker had followed all of the company regulations. If so, the worker was given a certificate, entitling the girl or boy to find work elsewhere. If the worker was not a suitable employee, no certificate was given, and the worker was blacklisted.

Some children resisted the working conditions and rules in subtle ways. Lucy Larcom, for instance, allowed herself a kind of escape by daydreaming as she worked. "I loved quietness," said Lucy. "I discovered that I could accustom myself to the noise, that it became like silence to me. And I defied the machinery to make me its slave. Its incessant discords could not drown the music of my thoughts if I let them fly high enough."

Other workers resisted by breaking the rules. Although factory regulations forbade books to be brought into the mills, many New England mill girls pasted poems, hymns, extracts of books, and mathematical problems on the windowsills or onto the sides of their looms or spinning frames. As the girls worked, they glanced at the papers, trying to memorize all they could. They also wrote on scraps of paper that they kept hidden in waste boxes. Tired as they were, some girls attended lectures and classes held at night. An education, they knew, might allow them to escape the mill forever.

Eventually the long hours, the drudgery, and the noisy machinery became too much for some. When Lucy Larcom quit, the paymaster asked if she were going where she would earn more money. "No," said Lucy. "I am going where I can have more time." Lucy loved to read and write poetry, to study botany and explorers. With the money she earned, she gained an education and went on to become a respected poet and teacher at Wheaton College.

"What Are We Coming To?"

The New England mill girls insisted that they were the social and intellectual equal of men and well-to-do girls who didn't work. In their "improvement circles," they produced stories, poetry, and essays. With help from local clergy and the mill owners, they published factory magazines such as *Lowell Offering* and *Factory Life. Lowell Offering* attracted national and international attention, as the girls received praise for their writing.

In the beginning, the girls used the magazines to show that mill girls were intelligent and capable of producing thoughtful work. However, as conditions worsened and salaries failed to rise, the girls used the magazines to reveal the unpleasant side of factory life—a side the owners wanted to keep hidden.

Lowell National Historical Park

The girls wrote stories that told of unbearable working conditions and the "evils of factory life." In their essays, the girls complained that the long workdays left no time "to cultivate the mind and form good habits." They also wrote letters that told about overseers who took advantage of female workers, forcing the girls "to abandon their virtue" to obtain favors. Other girls

Throughout the 1800s and into the 1900s, more mills and factories sprang up. These Georgia mill girls formed friendships just as the early New England mill girls did. Like Harriet Hanson, some girls became leaders. They organized their fellow workers to strike for improved labor conditions. Library of Congress

complained about the poor wages and compulsory church attendance. "Here I am, a healthy New England girl, quite well-behaved, bestowing just half of all my hours, including Sundays, upon a company for less than two cents an hour, and out of the other half of my time, I am obliged to wash, mend, read, reflect, go to church!!! . . . What are we coming to?"

As people read the magazines, they began to sympathize with the girls about the working conditions: the long hours, low pay, and limited leisure time. The public began to criticize factory owners and their exploitation of factory labor. There was no sadder sight, said some critics, than the thousands of mill girls on their way to and from work. Furthermore, some men decided that factory work ruined the health and the reputations of even the most worthy and virtuous girl.

Although the criticisms were valid in many ways, some people simply didn't believe that young women should work. They also didn't believe that women should vote or own property or manage their own money or study subjects like law, mathematics, or biology. Of course, the mill girls didn't agree, and men further worried about the independent spirit that developed in working girls.

CHAPTER TWO

"STICK TOGETHER AND WE'LL WIN"

Messenger, Bootblack, and Newsie Strike Fever New York City (1899)

"I grew up on a pool table," claimed Philip Marcus. "I lived on the streets practically all day, days and nights both. We used to sneak into the burlesque houses or the all-night places on West Madison Street and sleep there. The only trouble was that the ushers would come around and throw the flashlight in your face to see if you was awake. You wasn't supposed to go to sleep. Sometimes they threw us out."

Philip Marcus didn't really grow up on a pool table. When he was eight, he ran away from the Chicago tenement where he lived with his mother and two brothers. He supported himself by selling newspapers. Although he returned home from time to time, he spent most of his childhood living and working on the streets of Chicago, Illinois.

As cities grew, they changed the way children like Philip Marcus lived, worked, and played.

Many immigrants settled in major cities along the Atlantic seaboard or along major waterways. By 1870, the population of New York City was growing by fifty percent every ten years. Library of Congress

Reformers worried about the city dangers and lack of adult supervision for children who worked on city streets. Library of Congress

"Some of Us Had to Go"

Like Philip, some city kids left home and stayed away for days at a time. Another twelve-year-old Chicago boy and his seven friends slept in newspaper alleys or in large empty boxes. In the morning, when they awoke hungry, they scavenged for breakfast money. "We'd go out looking for barrels in alleys and backyards," said the boy. "We dumped out the garbage or trash and take them to a barrel factory to sell. . . . Having picked up a little money this way, we had breakfast."

When the police found the children, they often put them in jail while they

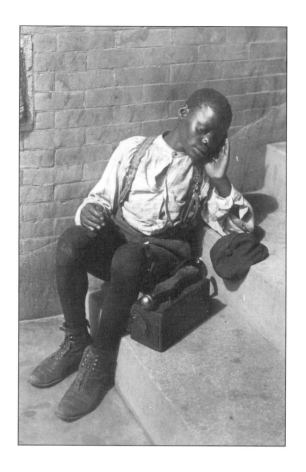

tried to locate the parents. One night the cops picked up Philip Marcus and his two younger brothers.

"It was the big roundup," said Philip. "Away we went to the cooler. The cops called up the old folks, and my mother came down to get us. She talked to the sergeant to lecture us so we'd come in off the streets at night. He made his lecture real good, but my mother got sore at me and only took Izzy and Manuel home. I was left there for two or three days."

Some parents didn't worry when their boys were missing, believing their children would return when they were hungry. Other parents were relieved when there was one less mouth to feed. "We was six," said another Chicago boy who lived on the streets and made money by shining shoes. "And we ain't got no father. Some of us had to go."

Although some adult reformers worried about the children, the children didn't seem worried. In the city, children always had something to do. They took over the streets and alleys, sidewalks and gutters, rooftops and fire escapes and vacant lots. Girls usually played jacks, jumped rope, bounced balls, and chanted rhymes, while boys played marbles, kick the can, leapfrog, and craps, a game of chance played with dice for money.

Boys played craps for money. Police often broke up the game. More children were arrested for gambling than any other offense. Photography Collection, University of Maryland Baltimore County

Like other children who worked, city kids were expected to hand their pay to their parents, who in return gave them a small amount to spend. In the early 1900s, a penny bought candy. A nickel bought a candy bar or a pass to a nickelodeon show. A dime or quarter seemed like a small fortune.

City kids also found plenty of ways to make money. They combed the dumps, scavenging for items to sell or use themselves. They collected papers, rags, and bottles to sell to the junkman for pennies. They found broken bicycles, wagons, and carriages and remodeled them into new toys. They picked bags of coal to bring home to their mothers to use or to sell.

"It's funny what crazy things a guy will do when money's important to

Children often spent Saturdays at the dumps, filling their sacks. They could sell two pounds of papers for a penny, one pound of rags for two cents, and a pound of copper for ten cents. Photography Collection, University of Maryland Baltimore County

him," said Philip Marcus. "I remember once my brother found a dollar bill on the floor of a saloon. I spent the rest of the night going in all of the saloons. I couldn't find a damn cent."

Some city kids, especially boys, formed gangs. Some gangs simply hung out together; others protected themselves from the neighborhood bully or guarded their territory from "outsiders." When boys were sent on errands outside their neighborhood, they usually carried small items to use as bribes if they were caught by rival gang members.

Gang members often stole petty items such as fruit or vegetables from pushcart vendors. They also stole milk and bread from the stoops of houses,

Gang members often plagued pushcart vendors by stealing fruit from their stands. Library of Congress

underwear and shirts from clotheslines on wash days, and even baby carriages—from right under the babies.

Some boys emptied delivery trucks and railroad cars. "I had a five-bushel wagon which we would load up with our 'haul,'" said one gang member. "Then we'd take it around to our regular customers. Lots of families stocked up that way."

Each gang had a leader, and members created and enforced their own rules. Their most basic code of honor was "no stooling," or telling on other gang members. "Anybody that snitched got sixty punches from each member of the gang," said one boy. "We beat him up hard." When a gang member was arrested, the boys often raised money to pay the fine.

"More Jobs Than I Could Do"

The growing cities thrived on the labor of children. The streets rang with the cries of kids who hawked newspapers, candy, and gum. Kids shined shoes, made deliveries, ran errands, and carried messages.

The city offered so much work that a kid could quit or get fired from one job and find a new job within hours. African-American children, often excluded from textile mills and factories, found work opportunities in the city. "I always had a job," said John Dobbs, who grew up in Savannah, Georgia. "Ever since I first worked as a delivery boy for the newspapers, I have had more jobs than I could do. If it wasn't the kind of work I liked, I did that until I could do better."

Although girls performed many of the same jobs as boys, more boys than girls worked in the street trades. Grown-ups wanted to protect girls from street dangers. They thought that girls learned little from selling newspapers, shining shoes, or delivering messages. Those jobs didn't prepare girls for marriage. City boys, on the other hand, needed to learn "street smarts."

Girls tended younger brothers or sisters while their mothers worked. Library of Congress

Consequently, most girls were destined to do laundry, iron, mend, sew, cook, clean, and run errands for their mothers. They picked over produce, haggled with grocers over day-old bread, and bargained with the butcher for better cuts of meat or a choice soup bone. When young girls weren't working by their mother's side, they minded their younger brothers and sisters while their mothers worked. They pushed their baby brothers and sisters in carriages or sat outside on the stoop to watch them play, often parking the carriages side by side.

Like John Dobbs, many boys held a variety of different jobs at the same time. In addition to peddling newspapers, for instance, Frank Andriole worked as a telegraph messenger boy and a bootblack.

"I was thirteen when I started delivering telegrams," said Frank. "I had a bicycle. I delivered telegrams after school, from four o'clock until eleven o'clock each night. . . . I also shined shoes on the ferryboats. From Staten Island to the Battery and back again. It was a forty-five minute run each way, and I could do five or six shines. Ten cents a shine, I got."

During the summer of 1899, the New York City boys who worked as messengers, bootblacks, and newsies became infused with strike fever. Newspaper reporters delighted in covering the strike stories. When they interviewed the boys or listened to their speeches, they enjoyed capturing their colorful language. They spelled the boys' words just as they sounded.

Although all three strikes weren't successful, the city saw how much power a group of determined boys could wield.

"With the Strikers Until the End"

In July 1899, New York City messenger boys were satisfied with their wages, but they weren't satisfied with other working conditions. The various telegraph companies all had similar policies regarding work shifts, fees for uniforms, and telegram delivery payment.

The messengers resented the unpredictable hours and the irregularity of their work: their shifts often changed from morning to afternoon to night with

This fourteen-year-old messenger worked until one o'clock in the morning every night. After work, he slept at the docks. On payday, his mother picked up his wages. Photography Collection, University of Maryland Baltimore County

only a day's notice. Some boys began at eight o'clock at night and were still there at ten the next morning. The boys wanted to work the same schedule for one continuous week.

The messenger boys were dissatisfied with the fees they were charged for their uniforms and white linen collars. The boys also had to pay for hats, rubber boots, and rubber coats.

"Mind yer," another boy told a *Sun* reporter, "they take fifty cents a week out for uniforms, and before yer wear one out, yer've paid for it a half dozen times over. But d'yer own it then? Not on yer life. They take it away, gives yer

In 1899, police didn't find it easy to control the striking messengers. According to a Sun *reporter, "A lot of small boys on strike are just as hard to handle as a lot of men."* Library of Congress

one that some large boys has grown out of, and keep right on taking yer fifty cents a week." The uniform, the boy figured, had cost the company only about five dollars, yet he had paid twenty-six dollars to wear it over the length of his employment.

The messenger companies paid only for telegrams that were delivered and accepted by the recipient. The boys wanted to be paid for each telegram they carried out of the office. To them, it wasn't fair to lose payment on messages just because the person addressed could not be found or refused to accept the message. This happened especially when the messages were from bill collectors.

When the companies refused to yield on their policies, the messenger boys declared a strike. They felt confident that a strike would cripple the city. How could Wall Street and other businesses survive without telegrams?

On July 22, a group of boys from the American District Messenger office sent a letter announcing their strike to the *New York Sun*. The newspaper printed the letter just as the boys wrote it, spelling and all:

> Gentlemen: We wish to inform you that the A.D.T. Stock Exchange boys of 314 Exchange court are going out on strick Monday. The cause of there stricking is they are charged by the company 50c a week the hole year round for the same uniform and 10c a week for collars which they say they ought to have for free. They also want to receive more money and in full pay TOO, nothing taking out if it for collars & uniforms as they are not worth it. They say the company does not do the right thing by them.
>
> Hoping to see this in your paper.
>
> Excuse writing.
>
> Boys of Dist. 3, 4, Ex. Court.

The American District Messenger office admitted that some of their messenger boys were "stirred up," but a company representative denied that any strike would take place. "It's all foolishness," he said. "There isn't any reason for the boys to strike." Another confident company official said they were prepared if the boys did strike: "We have one thousand boys in reserve," he claimed.

But the boys did strike. When the strikers saw reserve messengers, or "scabs," they chased them down the street. The captured scabs suffered beatings, which often convinced them to join the strike.

After strikers beat up one scab, the company boss, Mr. Henry Nichols, was outraged at the way his faithful employee had been treated. Mr. Nichols stepped outside "to lick a few of them" himself, but when he saw the crowd of striking boys, he quickly backed off.

Just as Mr. Nichols was retreating into the safety of his office, he noticed a familiar face. His own son was among the striking messenger boys! Furious, Mr. Nichols ordered his son to return to work "or take the worst thrashing he ever got."

But young Nichols refused to be a scab, no matter what kind of threats his father hurled at him. He yelled back to his father that he was "with the strikers until the end."

All in all, the messengers' strike was short-lived. It resulted in one dull morning at the Wall Street Stock Exchange, but otherwise, the strike did not paralyze the city as the boys had hoped.

The reason? The messengers had failed to organize and to rally under effective leadership. It was difficult to organize boys who worked for so many different companies, and there were too many reserve messengers. The strike fizzled a few days after it began. By July 27, telegraph message service resumed.

"Everybody Wasn't Poor"

New York City bootblacks also caught strike fever that same summer of 1899. Many bootblacks worked for men who owned several shoe-shine concession stands. Out of each dollar the boys earned, the boss kept sixty cents and the boys got forty. The tips, however, belonged to the boys.

Frank Andriole shined shoes on the ferryboats that ran from Staten Island to the Battery and back again. "The people who wanted shines were so well dressed," said Frank. "Some of them gave a good tip, too. They had the money to get their shoes shined rather than shine them themselves. I guess everybody wasn't poor."

Unlike the messenger boys, the East River ferry bootblacks succeeded in organizing an effective strike. The boys' main grievance came when their boss, Vincent Cataggio, installed cash registers. In an effort to keep the boys from cheating him, Cataggio required each shine to be rung up in the cash register.

The boys resented that their honesty was being questioned. They hated

Independent bootblacks bought their own polishes, usually black and brown.
Library of Congress

the cash register and its bell. The system was degrading, said the boys, because it made monkeys out of them.

"Of course, we go on a strike," one boy told a *Sun* reporter. "The boss, he make all the money, and he want to make the men ring up the shine like the monkey rings the bell in the circus. Next thing we know, he want to put a collar and chain on the men—same like Jocko [the monkey]."

The boys sent an ultimatum to Cataggio: either get rid of the cash registers or increase wages from five dollars to seven dollars a week. If he refused, the boys threatened to throw their stands off the ferries and into the water.

Cataggio agreed to a compromise. He kept the cash registers, but he offered the boys six dollars a week.

The boys accepted the one-dollar raise. "We've compromised," said a strike leader, "as we are not yet well organized." As soon as they were better organized, the leader promised, they would ask again for seven dollars.

Extra! Extra!

The most common job for city kids was selling newspapers. Some newsies were "street waifs," or boys who had run away from home. One reformer noted that several hundred newsies sleep out all night, on the streets, in stables, condemned buildings, and halls of tenements.

Most newsies, however, had homes to return to at night. They attended school during the day and sold newspapers at night and on the weekend. Although some girls hawked newspapers, the newsies were primarily boys, ranging in age from eight to fifteen.

To get started in their business enterprise, the newsies borrowed money from their parents, older brothers or sisters, or friends. In 1899, it cost fifty cents to buy one hundred newspapers, which sold for one cent.

The newsies thronged outside the newspaper offices, waiting for the papers, hot off the press. As they waited, they played games, threw balls in the street, pitched pennies, and played craps. They drank pop and ate candy, ice cream, and frankfurters. They also drank coffee and smoked cigarettes, which worried many adults.

Once the circulation managers threw open the office windows, the games were over. The paper rush began, and the playful boys became enterprising businessmen as they stepped up to the window to buy their newspapers from the manager.

In order to determine how many newspapers to buy, the newsie considered such factors as the importance of the headline, the time of day, day of week, season of year, weather conditions, and sports scores. He also considered his territory and how many papers he had sold the night before. Each newsie calculated carefully: leftover papers weren't refundable.

The newsies also developed aggressive marketing strategies. They shouted and pushed and elbowed. If the headlines weren't exciting enough to sell papers, they created headlines worth shouting.

"If there wasn't anything startling we could yell about to help sell the papers, we always got around it this way," said Philip Marcus. "We'd look

all over the sheet for a story from Washington, anything at all, no matter what it was, and then we'd yell: 'Read all about the White House scandal! The White House scandal! Read all about it!'"

To some, the newsies' embellishments created a real problem, especially when the boys exaggerated accounts about foreign wars. The made-up stories frightened people who had friends and relatives in the armed services. Some doctors believed that the newsies' constant shouting agitated people with nervous health problems.

Other people didn't like the newsies' coarse manners or the fact that the boys delighted in horrific headlines. The more war, murder, mayhem, and disaster, the happier the newsies seemed to be.

Reformers also grew alarmed at the newsies' keen knowledge of the city streets. The newsies knew the city well, and they became notorious as a good source of information. "You could find out from us almost anything you wanted to know," said Philip Marcus. "Where the saloons were, the location of the gambling joints, the whorehouses, almost anything." The boys frequented the bars and saloons to sell papers to drunks. They knew that drunks often tipped generously.

The city became the newsies' home, workplace, and playground. These newsies are catching goldfish in a fountain. Library of Congress

Newsies also preyed on the customer's sympathy. They often pretended to be poor, hungry, ill, or injured in the hope that an unsuspecting customer would give a larger tip or buy an extra paper. A few softies bought the entire bundle.

For some newsies, the injuries were real. Newsboys often "flipped" cars, meaning they jumped aboard moving trains or streetcars for a free ride. Sometimes the newsboys fell from the cars and onto the track. They lost their arms or legs when the wheels ran over them.

One woman, distressed at the number of maimed newsboys, created a fund to raise money to buy wooden legs. But the newsboys didn't want wooden legs. They knew that a crutch and empty pant leg evoked far more sympathy—and tips—from customers.

Many kids had few scruples when it came to making money. They often developed "dodges" or tricks to cheat customers. If a customer appeared har-

Newsies "flipped" streetcars. Once aboard, they hawked their papers up and down the aisle. Photography Collection, University of Maryland Baltimore County

ried, the newsie took his time fumbling for change, hoping the customer would be too impatient to wait.

The newsie could also cheat customers who weren't paying attention. While waiting for change, an inattentive customer might get three pennies instead of four. "Nine times out of ten, he sticks the pennies in his pocket without looking at them," said Philip Marcus. "And that's the dodge."

Some boys waited at streetcar stops to sell to the passengers, using the stops as another opportunity to cheat customers. "We used to run up alongside the car and the people in the car would stick their hands through the windows for a paper," said Philip Marcus. "If he gave us a nickel or a dime, it was just too bad, we'd fumble and we'd fumble—boy, we sure had to dig deep for that change—and we'd even run alongside the car when it started out, but—it never failed—we just couldn't reach him. The car would be

Girl newsies were not as common as boys. When cities set age limits, they often established a higher minimum age for girls than boys. In some states, girls had to be sixteen to sell newspapers, but boys only had to be ten. Library of Congress

picking up speed and we just couldn't reach his hand with that change." Sometimes the cheated customers got off the streetcar at the next stop and returned for their change. "They were wised up," said Philip. "Or maybe they sold papers once themselves."

The older newsies usually "owned" the best spots—their own territory or corner—to sell papers. "Every busy corner was held down by some big guy," said Philip Marcus. "Us little kids, we ran around the streets; we wasn't allowed to sell on any of those corners."

After the paper rush subsided, the older boys sometimes struck deals with the younger newsies to buy their leftover papers. "One of the big guys would say to one of the little guys, 'Hey, punk, want to buy me out tonight?'" said Philip Marcus. "An' the little guy said yes. It was his ass if he didn't."

Some of the younger boys looked forward to the chance to sell papers in a good spot, but most were simply afraid to refuse the bigger boys. "I made a deal with a guy," said Philip Marcus. "I said I'd buy him out. But when I looked at all the papers he had left, there was more than I thought I could sell. But there wasn't two ways about it. I had to buy them and I did. I started to bawl. And while I was standing there bawling, I sold all them sheets."

"Kill De Guy Wot Sells De Xtras"

Throughout the 1880s and 1890s, the newspaper industry boomed. Millionaire publishers such as William Randolph Hearst, who owned the *New York Journal,* and Joseph Pulitzer, who owned the *New York World,* enjoyed tremendous success. They continued to invest money in their newspapers, creating splashy headlines and putting out extra editions.

But by 1899, the huge profits tapered off. Although Hearst and Pulitzer competed with each other, they both wanted to recover their investments. They considered raising the cost of their newspapers, but they feared that customers would buy other papers instead.

Hearst and Pulitzer were shrewd businessmen. If they couldn't charge the customers more, they could recover their losses by charging the newsies more. And so they did. They raised the cost of the wholesale price that the newsboys paid for the papers. The cost of the paper for the customer remained the same, but the newsies' cost increased from fifty cents to sixty cents for one hundred papers.

The difference was only ten cents, but if ten cents meant that much to millionaires like Hearst and Pulitzer, it meant even more to the newsies. The angry newsboys demanded that the owners roll back the price increase—or they would boycott the *Journal* and *World.*

Pulitzer and Hearst refused. No boys were going to tell them how to run their business or threaten them with a strike.

On Wednesday, July 19, the downtown New York City newsboys gathered in City Hall Park. They announced that their strike would take place the next day. The newsboys elected officers, formed a committee on discipline, determined a strike strategy, and sent out delegates to spread the word to other newsies in other parts of the city. They also sent word to newsies in Harlem, Brooklyn, Long Island City, and Jersey City: no newsie should sell the *Journal* and *World* until their demand for a price rollback was met.

The newsies were led by Kid Blink, a boy described as small for his age and having only one eye. He told the boys that success was possible if they held together. "We've got the uptown boys, the Long Island and City boys, and the Brooklyn boys with us," said Kid Blink. "If we can get the advertisers with us, we win in a walk. Anyway, we're going to hold out."

Within a few days, the strike spread from Manhattan to Brooklyn to Harlem to Battery Park and across the rivers to Long Island City and Newark. It even affected cities in New Jersey, Connecticut, Massachusetts, and Rhode Island.

As could be expected, competing newspapers didn't feel sorry for Hearst and Pulitzer. The *New York Sun,* the *Brooklyn Eagle,* the *New York Times,* and others reveled in the boycott. Captivated by the boys' antics, spunk, and determination, the reporters cheered them on, covering the strike in great detail.

The newsies erected placards near the Brooklyn Bridge that said: "Kill De

Newsies often hawked papers outside theaters, department stores, and churches.
Photography Collection, University of Maryland Baltimore County

Guy Wot Sells De Xtras." They took up a collection and had handbills printed, which they passed out to pedestrians. The handbills read: "Help us in our struggle to get fair play by not buying the *Journal* or the *World.* Help us! Do not ask for the *Journal* or the *World.*" Sympathetic pedestrians threw small change at the boys.

As they promised, the striking boys treated scabs roughly. The boys, armed with stones and other missiles, waited at various points throughout the city for the newspaper delivery wagons. They cried "Soak him! Soak him!" and bombarded the drivers with ammunition. They tore bundles of papers and littered the streets.

The boys didn't care if the fight wasn't fair. Throughout the strike, they outnumbered and attacked many scabs. But they wouldn't attack the women who owned their own stands and continued to sell the boycotted newspapers. "A feller can't soak a lady," explained Kid Blink.

At left: Joseph Pulitzer owned the New York World, *which the newsies boycotted in 1899. Today Pulitzer is remembered for the number of monetary prizes and scholarships he endowed for distinction in journalism, letters, and music.*
At right: William Randolph Hearst created a chain of popular newspapers, noted for their sensational reporting. In 1899, when newsies boycotted the Journal, *competing newspapers compared the newsies' strike to the story of David and Goliath.* Library of Congress

On July 22, Kid Blink and several other newsies waited for William Hearst outside the *Journal* office building. When he arrived in a cab, the smallest newsie approached him, and said, "We're the strikers, Mr. Hearst."

Hearst said, "Well, boys, what can I do for you?"

"We want one hundred papers for fifty cents," said the boy.

Hearst invited four boys into his office to discuss the matter. Kid Blink, Dave Simons, and two other boys followed Hearst inside. When they returned, Kid Blink reported that Hearst would give the boys an answer on Monday, July 24.

But on Monday, the boys discovered that Hearst and Pulitzer didn't give in. The two publishers had hired several hundred "men and big strapping boys" at two dollars a day to sell the *Journal* and *World.*

The newsies retaliated by raiding newsstands and emptying delivery trucks. They also "kicked up, tripped, and buffeted" the scabs. In one instance, a reporter said that six men went down like "tender stalks before a cyclone."

Police were called to the scenes, but somehow, the police usually arrived moments after the attacks were over and the newspapers were shredded. One reporter claimed that the police didn't seem too eager to catch the boys.

That evening, on July 24, newspaper reporters covered a mass meeting of more than five thousand striking newsboys at New Irving Hall on Broome Street. Two thousand boys crammed inside the building, and the remaining three thousand thronged outside.

The meeting lasted two hours. The newsies listened to speeches by other newsies and supportive adults. When Kid Blink spoke, he told the boys: "I'm here to say that if we are going to win the strike, we must stick together like glue and never give in. Am I right?"

"Soak 'em, Blink," a boy from the audience yelled.

The two thousand boys inside the hall cheered and applauded. Although they couldn't hear Kid Blink, the crowd of boys outside the hall cheered, too.

"I'm trying to figure out how ten cents on a hundred can mean more to a millionaire than it does to a newsboy. I can't see it." Kid Blink went on to ask the boys to curtail the violence. "I don't believe in hitting the drivers of the news wagons. I don't believe in dumping the carts, same as was done in Madison Street last night. I'll tell you the truth. I was one of the boys that did it, but it ain't right." Kid Blink concluded by promising the boys a "monster parade."

After the speeches, the boys sang songs. When the meeting ended, a reporter said that the boys "howled like demons" and ran out of the hall. The newsies spent the rest of the evening celebrating and looking forward to their monster parade.

Traitors!

After the newsboys' meeting, the strikers made fewer attacks on the drivers and delivery wagons. But Kid Blink's promise of a parade went unfulfilled. Another strike leader, Dave Simons, assured the boys that a parade would take place on July 27. He promised three bands: "One for the Manhattan boys, one for the Brooklyn boys, and one for the Harlem boys." To reporters, he announced that six thousand newsboys would line up at eight o'clock in front of city hall.

On July 27, two hundred boys waited eagerly in front of city hall, but neither Dave Simons nor Kid Blink showed up. Rumors began to circulate that Hearst and Pulitzer had bought them off.

At last, Kid Blink and Dave Simons appeared. They claimed that the enemy—the *Journal* and *World* newspapers—started the traitor rumors in an attempt to turn the newsies against one another. But the parade never took place. The leaders postponed it once again.

The boys were growing disappointed in their leaders. They held their own meeting to discuss the problem and renew their pledge. They gave speeches and passed a cigar box for contributions to the strike fund. To a *Sun* reporter, they vowed that their fight could last indefinitely because "We ain't got no wifes and families."

The next day, July 28, the *World* and *Journal* advertised again for men to sell papers. Seven hundred men responded. Determined to teach the boys a lesson, both publishers announced that they would not back down. Don Seitz, the business manager for the *World,* declared that both newspapers "would not recede from their position." He said that there would be no reduction on the price charged for the *World* and that the *Journal* would also maintain the rates.

Meanwhile, the newsies couldn't find their leaders, Kid Blink and Dave Simons, but they managed to carry on the strike, despite Hearst's and Pulitzer's strong-arm tactics. "Not a copy of the proscribed papers could be bought in any part of the district," claimed the *Brooklyn Eagle.*

Although reformers worried about the children who worked on city streets, many newsies developed a gritty self-reliance. The streets taught them lessons they didn't learn in school. Library of Congress

Finally, a large group of newsies discovered Dave Simons and several older boys carrying bundles of the *Journal* and the *World.* To the newsies' dismay, the rumors about their leaders proved true after all.

Furious, the boys mobbed Simons and his friends. The police arrived, brandishing nightsticks, but the boys kept on fighting. They swept the police off their feet, said a reporter, and "swarmed about them like ants . . . worried them front and rear." More police responded, but it was too late. The boys had already destroyed six thousand newspapers.

At that moment, the mob of boys spotted Kid Blink. He was wearing a new

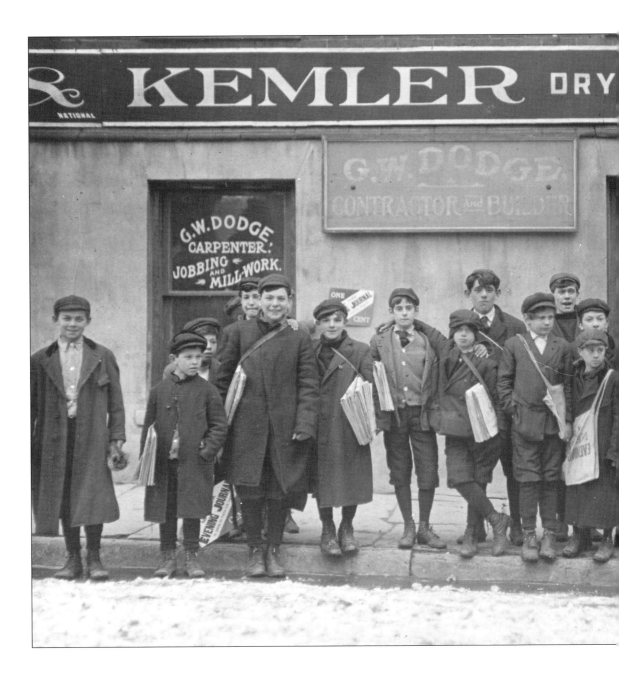

suit of clothes. The boys concluded that Kid Blink had been bought off as well. Consumed with anger, they closed in about him, calling him a traitor. Kid Blink denied their accusations, but the boys didn't believe him. Realizing the danger, he turned and ran down the street. Yelling, the newsies chased him.

Luckily for Kid Blink, two detectives turned the corner and saw him running. They also saw the rush of boys behind him. The detectives assumed, incorrectly, that Kid Blink was leading the mob. They caught him and arrested him on the spot, probably saving him from an attack. No one knows what the boys would have done if they had gotten to Kid Blink first.

Kid Blink was taken to jail, where he was identified as Louis Ballatt. One of the boycotted newspapers offered to bail him out, but his bail was paid by his mother.

At last, Hearst and Pulitzer conceded defeat. According to a memo from the *World*'s Don Seitz to his boss, Joseph Pulitzer, the loss in circulation had been "colossal." The press run had been reduced by two-thirds.

Hearst and Pulitzer struck a compromise with the boys. The wholesale price of the *Journal* and *World* would remain at sixty cents for one hundred papers, but both newspapers agreed to refund the cost of all unsold newspapers.

The boys accepted the partial victory. On August 2, their two-week strike ended. Once again, the newsies played ball and craps, drank pop and coffee, ate frankfurters and smoked cigarettes as they waited in line to buy their supply of *Journal*s and *World*s.

CHAPTER THREE

"DEAR GOD, WILL IT EVER BE DIFFERENT?"

Pauline Newman and the New York City Rent Strike (1907)

In the summer of 1907, sixteen-year-old Pauline Newman lost her job. A severe economic depression had gripped New York City, causing hundreds of garment factories to lay off their workers. More than one hundred thousand people were out of work.

Many workers panicked. How could they buy food for their families? Pay for doctors? Pay their rent? They feared they would be evicted from their tenement apartments.

Wash fluttered on clotheslines high above the tenement yards. Library of Congress

But Pauline Newman and several other young women from the Triangle Shirtwaist Factory looked at the crisis as an opportunity. She and her friends took their bedrolls and a rented tent to the Palisades, the high white cliffs that overlooked the Hudson River. There, among the grass and trees, they set up camp for the summer.

"Thus we avoided paying rent or, worse still, being evicted," Pauline later recalled. "Besides which, we liked living in the open—

plenty of fresh air, sunshine, and the lovely Hudson for which there was no charge."

Pauline and her friends didn't miss the stifling factory and the whir, groan, and grind of machinery. "We enjoyed the cool of the evening, glorious sunsets, the moon and the stars," said Pauline.

During those summer months, the girls found odd jobs and pooled their money to buy food. Years later, Pauline recalled how they ate bread, cake, and "beans, beans, beans." They also hiked, read, and sang around the campfire at night.

The girls sat up late many nights. They talked about their shared experiences: their bosses, the long hours, the low pay, their lives in the Lower East Side tenements. "I lived on Madison Street in one of the tenements," said Pauline. "Tenements without facilities . . . no bathing facilities, no bathroom, no toilet. The toilet was in the yard."

When fall came, the factories called the girls back to work. Pauline and her friends rolled up their blankets, packed their tents, and moved back to the tenements. Their lives seemed to return to normal.

But later that fall, the tenement landlords announced an increase in the rent. Pauline and her friends considered the rent increase unjust. It wasn't fair to be expected to pay more rent when the landlords weren't making improvements.

The girls decided to organize a protest against the rent increase. They named sixteen-year-old Pauline Newman leader of the rent strike.

"A Horrible Experience"

In 1901, Pauline Newman was nine when she immigrated with her mother and two older sisters to the United States from Lithuania, Russia. Years later, she recalled the journey: "It was a horrible experience. Only I didn't know enough to know it was horrible."

During the two-week voyage, many immigrants became sick in the cramped steerage section of the steamship, the space allotted to the lowest-paying passengers. The steerage section reeked of dampness, unwashed bodies, and vomit. Each day, the immigrant passengers had only tea, soup, bread, and jam to eat.

Pauline missed her Lithuanian village: her low thatched cottage, the marketplace, the woods and wildflowers, and the lake where she often swam and skated.

Pauline Newman, her two sisters, and her mother are pictured here in Lithuania, Russia, shortly before her father died. Nine-year-old Pauline is seated in front, holding a book.
Elisabeth Burger

When the Newmans landed at Ellis Island, they discovered that all of their luggage was missing. "Nice things—copper utensils, handmade things, we never got it," said Pauline. "We were told to come again and again, and we did and it was useless. In the luggage was our Bible. On the flyleafs of our Bible was the birth dates of the children."

Many immigrants could afford to travel only in the crowded and unsanitary conditions of the steerage section of the steamship. Library of Congress

Pauline, her mother, and her two sisters settled into a tenement apartment in the Lower East Side, the immigrant section of New York City, where more than six hundred factories offered work opportunities. Employers found a steady stream of immigrant men, women, and children willing to accept harsh working and living conditions.

Blocks and blocks of tenements offered housing to immigrants. The tenements were dull red brick or wooden buildings, usually seven to nine stories high. The buildings had narrow entranceways, dingy and unlighted. The stairs were rickety and the halls were dark. Narrow alleys between buildings led to rear tenements and small shops.

Most landlords didn't take good care of the tenements, and practically all the buildings were firetraps, unsafe and in poor condition. Because the landlords wanted to make as much money as they could as quickly as possible, the buildings were not constructed soundly. Rain dripped through the apartment ceilings. Wind and dirt blew through cracks in the walls. Fire escapes were often blocked.

To help make ends meet, families took in boarders, and several families sometimes shared a three-room apartment designed for just one family. The families hung calico sheets to divide the rooms. Children slept anywhere—in the living room or the kitchen, even tied to a chair so they wouldn't fall over.

A group of newly arrived immigrants wait to be processed at Ellis Island.
Library of Congress

Immigrants joked that people who lived in tenements got only two good baths throughout their lives—one from the midwife when they were born and one from the undertaker when they died. Library of Congress

They shared beds with siblings or boarders. Often, people slept in shifts: those who worked at night took turns using the beds with those who worked during the day. In summer, when the air was too hot and too heavy to breathe, entire families slept on the rooftops or on the fire escapes.

Several families usually shared one toilet, located in a small closet in the hallway of the building. Or they shared a privy in the backyard. Some tenements had a community faucet located on each floor.

Throughout the tenement districts, sewers were often clogged, streets and alleys littered with garbage. Sheds and shacks were squeezed onto every available space.

Yet tenement families were considered fortunate compared to others who didn't have a tiny, cramped apartment. Families who couldn't afford the rent lived at the dumps in shacks constructed out of old boards and oilcloth. Stables, cellars, and attics became homes. Some families couldn't afford to stay together. Brothers and sisters were sent to orphanages.

"A Common Understanding"

Once the Newmans arrived in New York and settled into their apartment, Pauline's two older sisters found work as seamstresses. When Pauline turned ten, she found a job assembling hairbrushes in a factory. She worked ten and a half hours Monday through Friday, and nine hours on Saturdays.

When the factory closed down, Pauline found another job making cigarettes. She earned twenty-five cents a day and a ten-cent bonus if she made a set amount beyond the required number. Eager for the bonus, she made so many extra cigarettes that she was fired. "I was told that until all the cigarettes on hand had sold, I was not needed," said Pauline.

She next found a job sewing buttons on shirtwaists. The tailored blouses and dresses were a popular clothing item for women during the early 1900s. Pauline quit this job when she found a better offer at the Triangle Shirtwaist Company, one of the largest factories in the Lower East Side. There, she joined the youngest children working in the "kindergarten corner," where she cut and trimmed threads from unfinished garments.

"[We] worked from seven-thirty to six-thirty at night when it wasn't busy," said Pauline. "When the season was on, we worked until nine o'clock. No overtime pay." To help pass the time as they worked, the children played games, told stories, and sang songs. One of their favorite songs was "I Would Rather Sleep Than Eat."

During the rush season, a sign was posted every Saturday afternoon, for all employees to see. The sign read: "If you don't come in Sunday, don't come in Monday." The children and the adults were required to work seven days a week or they would lose their jobs. This meant working eighty hours a week for no extra pay. Instead of overtime pay, the girls were given apple turnovers to eat during the extra hours.

Throughout the tenement districts, garbage and refuse littered the streets. When a horse dropped dead from heat exhaustion or other causes, the carcass might not be carted away for days. Library of Congress

The older girls, the sewers, weren't allowed to talk as they worked. Pauline remembered how the bosses wore noiseless rubber-heeled shoes: "You never knew when they [the bosses] would sneak up on you, spying to be sure you did not talk to each other during work hours."

By 1901, New York had laws that restricted young children from working at night. But the laws didn't deter the factory bosses. Many bosses were tipped off when a factory inspector was coming. If an inspector stopped by to check for underage child workers, the bosses had enough advance warning to tell the children to hide.

"We children would climb into the big box the finished shirts were stored in," said Pauline Newman. "Then some shirts were piled on top and when the inspector came—no children." To the children, it was great fun to hide from the inspectors.

The bosses often felt they were helping families. "If boys and girls were big and strong enough to work, even if they were a little under the legal age, I gave them a chance to keep their jobs," said Philippe LeMay, a foreman in a Lawrence, Massachusetts, mill. "Their parents were poor and needed every cent they could get. So I'd tell these younger workers to keep out of sight until the inspector had gone away. There was no harm to anybody and it did a lot of good."

Yet harm *was* being done to the children. Even as a young child, Pauline Newman understood the harm. Each day, as she walked home from work, she was filled with an overwhelming sadness as she saw the faces of tired workers.

One day, Pauline saw a young boy selling a newspaper called the *Jewish Daily Forward.* She bought the paper. She later described the first piece that caught her attention: "[It] was a story about working men and women of the East Side, the conditions under which they lived and worked—the long hours, the terribly low wages, the filthy tenements."

Pauline read other stories about the people around her, immigrants like herself who worked and lived the way she did. She also read the work of Yiddish poets and ideas about political theory and socialism. She became so interested that she couldn't wait to buy the next copy of the paper.

Day after day, Pauline bought and read the *Daily Forward.* It inspired her to write an article about the discouragement she felt over her drab existence, the lonely men and women, the hopeless faces and tired eyes. "Dear God," she wrote, "will it ever be different?"

She sent her article to the *Daily Forward.* "I did not think it was good enough for publication," said Pauline. "I just wanted to express my feelings and get them down on paper. I posted the article and did not give it another thought."

A few days later, her co-workers held up the newspaper and pointed to her article. "They all shouted congratulations and hailed me as a conquering hero," she said. "I could hardly believe it! But there was my name and all."

Encouraged by her success, she continued to write poems, articles, and stories about the living and working conditions that existed in the Lower East Side. Throughout her teenage years, she was a regular contributor to the *Jewish Daily Forward.*

In 1904, thirteen-year-old Pauline joined the newly formed New York Women's Trade Union League, a group committed to organizing working women into trade unions and lobbying for better wages, shorter work hours, and safer working conditions. She made friends with women labor leaders such as Rose Schneiderman. She often gave speeches on street corners and in front of factories to continue working girls to join the union.

By the time Pauline turned fourteen, she worked in the sewing room of the Triangle Shirtwaist Factory, where hundreds of teenage girls and young women sat at long rows of tables and sewed pieces of shirtwaists. Some girls sewed cuffs, while others sewed collars, yokes, buttonholes, sleeves, or pleated front panels. It took ten girls to make one shirtwaist. Men also worked in the factory, but they were given the higher-paid jobs of cutters (the workers who cut the cloth) or bosses.

Pauline Newman learned a lot from her experiences living in the tenements and working with women on the shop floor. She understood why people didn't just quit jobs, despite deplorable working conditions. For one reason, work wasn't always easy to find, and the same conditions existed in most factories.

People stayed for emotional reasons, too. "One gets used to a place, even if it is only a workshop," explained Pauline. "One gets to know the people you work with. You are no longer a stranger and alone. You have a feeling of

"Home work" meant sewing unfinished garments at home. Even the youngest children were trained to pull basting threads, sew buttons, string beads, embroider lace, or make cigarettes, hair brushes, powder puffs, or other small items. Photography Collection, University of Maryland Baltimore County

belonging, which helps make life in a factory a bit easier to endure. Very often friendships are formed and a common understanding established."

In 1907, sixteen-year-old Pauline Newman counted on this idea of common understanding to draw the tenants together. Her years of work experience taught her that many women and girls shared the same hopes and dreams for their futures and the futures of their families, regardless of their background. This "common understanding" would form the backbone of the rent strike.

Each morning, this twelve-year-old girl and her brother walked to the factory loft and picked up the day's sewing to do at home. Photography Collection, University of Maryland Baltimore County

"The New Joan of Arc"

It wasn't the first time that the landlords in New York had raised the rent. Previously, most tenement families responded to rent increases by moving, sometimes as many as three or four times in one year.

By 1904, however, moving was difficult. The city had torn down many buildings to make room to build the Williamsburg Bridge, a new school, and several parks in the Lower East Side. Thousands of families had little choice when their landlords raised the rent: there was no place to move.

"The landlords can afford to laugh," said Victor Rousseau, a reporter. "For every tenant who might depart, fifty more come crowding through the gates of Ellis Island."

As leader of the rent protest, Pauline Newman knew she needed to organize and mobilize the tenants. She understood the importance of coalition—uniting for a common goal. Instead of organizing against employers, Pauline Newman and the other residents of the Lower East Side needed to unite against the rent increase.

To the tenants, their case seemed strong. From 1905 to 1907, the average rent had increased thirty-three percent. The cost of a two-room apartment had risen from fifteen dollars to twenty. The tenants wanted their rent decreased by eighteen to twenty percent, which amounted to about two dollars a month. "When you are hungry and out of work," said one East Side resident, "two dollars is something big. And in twelve months, the savings will more than pay a whole month's rent. Two dollars cut off the rent right now will buy a good deal to eat."

By December 26, Pauline and her friends had organized four hundred working girls. In the evening, the girls went door-to-door throughout the tenement apartments in the Lower East Side. They explained the strike and convinced mothers and housewives to join in the protest. The recruits then canvassed the rest of the neighborhood during the day. All in all, more than ten thousand families promised to join in the rent strike, and newspapers hailed Pauline Newman as "The New Joan of Arc."

The housewives already knew about protests. In the past, the women had campaigned against the high cost of food. When the cost of kosher meat had gone up fifty percent, thousands of women marched through the streets of the Lower East Side. They entered kosher butcher shops and threw the meat into the streets. They staged a boycott and patrolled the shops to make sure no one patronized them. The women won: the price was rolled back to within two cents of its original cost.

Sixteen-year-old Cecilla Arkin and thirty-two-year-old Florence Margolies joined Pauline. Once the three leaders organized the network of groups, the rent protest grew on its own. A newspaper reporter said: "So effectively has [Pauline Newman] worked, that not only has she solidified the lower section, but she has found time to carry the war uptown."

The leaders sent word to the landlords: lower the rent or the tenants would refuse to pay. The tenants set a deadline of January 2, 1908, the day the landlords would collect the new rent.

The striking tenants were prepared. The Socialist party promised to provide legal aid and temporary housing for any family that faced eviction. The tenants knew that eviction would be costly for the landlords—as much as eight dollars per family to process the necessary paperwork. Certainly, the strikers believed, the landlords would concede and roll back the rent.

The strikers decorated their buildings with American flags and red Socialist flags. They posted large signs over doorways, which announced, "We Are Striking Here for Lower Rent" and "This Building Is on Strike" and "We Defy Anyone to Rent an Apartment Here."

They also threatened to report the many safety and housing violations in most tenements. The tenants knew that the landlords wouldn't want to invest in the required improvements.

By December 28, when the landlords still hadn't conceded, the tenants made lists of all the building code violations and presented them to city officials. Soon the East Side was filled with inspectors from the Tenement House Department and the Health Department. The inspectors examined the plumbing and fire escapes, and measured the air shafts between buildings. They also counted the number of families living on each floor. When they were done, the inspectors posted notices on buildings that failed the inspection. The landlords would be required to fix the problems.

Real estate agents from other sections of the city appeared in the Lower East Side, trying to lure the tenants away to other areas of New York City. But the tenants didn't want to relocate. The East Side was their home—where their relatives and friends lived, where their synagogues and churches were located. For many, it would have been too expensive to commute from another neighborhood to the clothing and cloak factories where they worked.

The rent strikers printed thousands of leaflets and scattered them throughout the East Side. Most were written in Yiddish, the language of the majority

Pauline Newman (right) and her fellow strike leaders counted on "common understanding" to form the backbone of the rent strike. New York Evening Journal, December 31, 1907

of residents. In the leaflets, the strikers urged the tenants to stick together. The tenants had the power, said the strikers, to wage a successful war against "landlord leeches." If the landlords tried to evict the striking tenants, blocks and blocks would be filled with furniture. No landlord would want that, for it would represent all the rent they were losing. The leaflets also called for a mass meeting of the tenants.

Some landlords sympathized with their tenants but still resented the strike. One landlord admitted that he would reduce the rent if the tenants came to him quietly and asked. "It is hard to fill vacated rooms," said J. A. Wasserman, a dentist. "I'd rather lower the rent a dollar where I am pressed

Tenants did not want to pay more for their housing, especially when landlords didn't take good care of the buildings. Photography Collection, University of Maryland Baltimore County

Children helped their families make ends meet by scavenging materials to use or to sell. Photography Collection, University of Maryland Baltimore County

than lose a family. But I will not be scared into doing it." Some landlords offered to reduce the monthly rent by fifty cents but said they would not consider a two-dollar reduction.

Other landlords weren't as sympathetic. One landlord became furious that strikers were talking to the tenants in his building. "Who has been going through my house working up those people?" he shouted at a committee of strikers. "If I catch anybody else running through my houses doing that, I'll shoot them."

A committee of strikers visited New York City Police Commissioner Theodore Bingham to discuss the rent problem and police brutality. To their dismay, the commissioner sided with the landlords. "If you don't like your rents, get out," Commissioner Bingham reportedly told them. "If you are not satisfied with our system of rents, go back where you came from."

Only Nine Evictions in the Rent Strike

EVICTED TENANTS AT NO. 179 MONROE STREET.

Hundreds of Dispossess Warrants Not Executed Indicate Settlements and Compromises While Both Sides Are Claiming Victory—Mrs. Stokes Sees Object Lesson in Tenants' Fight.

New York *Herald,* January 9, 1908

A mass meeting was held on December 29. The speakers urged the tenants to stand together in the fight. Again they reminded the tenants that the landlords would find it more advantageous to reduce the rent than to evict families.

Despite the tenants' determination, the landlords refused to back down. The landlords had the law on their side. "A rent strike cannot be entertained as an excuse for not paying the rent," declared one judge.

On January 2, the landlords sent out agents to collect the rent, and by January 7 they served eviction notices to six thousand of the ten thousand striking families. The notice gave the families three days to pay their rent or they would be evicted.

The landlords believed the tenants would quickly pay the rent when they saw police officers tossing their furniture out onto the street. As one family was evicted, the children clutched their mother's long skirt while she shouted and motioned wildly at the policemen. But the mother didn't give in. Instead of paying rent, she and the children picked up their belongings—a three-legged table, two broken chairs, a heap of garments, a bed, crockery, and a stove, warm and still hissing—and moved in with neighbors.

Some striking tenants, faced with eviction, did offer to pay their rent, but the landlords evicted them anyway. "Some of them came running around today to pay their rents," said one landlord. "But I wouldn't accept the money and will put them out. They cause me more trouble than their rent is worth."

"I Became Famous"

The rent strike resulted in reduced rents for approximately two thousand families. For some, this represented failure, but others disagreed. "It has jolted the rent system, perhaps beyond recovery," declared Victor Rousseau.

The rent strike drew reformers together from all classes—the wealthy, the middle class, and the working class—to improve neighborhoods in big-city slum areas. They lobbied for rent to be capped at thirty percent of a worker's income. But rent control was difficult to win; it took over twenty years for the passage of rent control laws.

Still, despite the small gains, a sixteen-year-old named Pauline Newman had initiated and mobilized thousands of tenants. "I became famous," said Pauline. "I was invited to speak at meetings which provided an opportunity for self-expression and the art of speaking in public."

These experiences helped Pauline develop into a fierce and eloquent labor leader. For the rest of her life, Pauline Newman fought for the rights of working women.

CHAPTER FOUR

"I'LL BE A JOHNNY MITCHELL MAN"

The Anthracite Coal Strikes Pennsylvania (1897, 1900, and 1902)

In the anthracite coal region of Pennsylvania, the breaker whistle called the boys and men to work at the colliery before dawn. Its thin icy blast could be heard more than eight miles away.

The youngest boys worked at the breaker, where the coal was broken, cleaned, and sorted for market. "We went to work in a bunch," said Joseph Gedrimas, a former breaker boy. "It was quite a sight to see us going to work with our dinner pails almost dragging to the ground."

By 1885, Pennsylvania law forbade boys younger than twelve to work in the breakers and forbade boys younger than fourteen to work

Breaker boys carried tin lunch pails just like their fathers. Stephen N. Lukasik

inside the mines. But parents found it easy to get around the state laws: they simply wrote on the work certificates the age they wanted their sons to be. This way, young boys were passed off as "small for twelve or fourteen." The breaker boss did the hiring and firing. To him, all that mattered was whether a boy was big enough and fit enough to work.

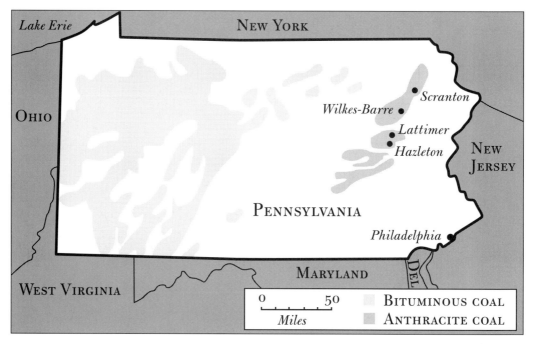

Four anthracite coal fields are located in the eastern region of Pennsylvania. At its peak in 1917, anthracite production reached 100 million tons annually. People preferred to heat their homes with anthracite coal, which was less smoky and produced more heat than the softer bituminous coal.

Lessons from the Breaker

The breaker boys worked from seven in the morning until six or six-thirty at night. All day, they sat hunched over the coal chutes, picking out the slate and other useless material mixed in with the coal.

The breaker boss watched the boys carefully. He carried a stick or broom that he used to probe blocked coal chutes or to jab boys who daydreamed, fell asleep, talked, or performed slow or careless work. "If you let some rock go through," said Joe Sudol, "he would poke you in the back with a stick."

By quitting time, the boys' backs ached. The fingers of new breaker boys developed a painful condition called "red tips." The sulfur deposits on the coal and slate irritated the boys' skin. Their fingers swelled, cracked open, and bled. After a few weeks, the boys' skin toughened up.

The breaker boss often found it difficult to manage the spirited breaker boys.
Wyoming Historical and Geological Society

Yet the boys managed to resist the harsh working conditions. They often teased the breaker boss by throwing pieces of rock at him when he turned his back. Sometimes they threw pieces of wood into the machinery, causing it to break down. While men repaired the machinery, the boys played games.

The boys also learned the value of sticking together, and sometimes they protested by organizing wildcat strikes. During such strikes, they refused to work until their demands were met. At one breaker, for instance, the boys struck when the coal company bosses canceled the annual winter sledding party.

The bosses tried to prevent the boys from striking. If the breaker wasn't working, the coal couldn't be processed. A breaker boy strike could shut down the entire colliery operation.

At a Pottsville breaker, the bosses blocked the doorway to stop the boys from swarming out. Several boys climbed to the rafters and kicked coal dust

Despite the hard work, the boys had fun whenever they could get away with it. Charles Kumpas

down on the bosses. A black cloud filled the air, making it difficult to see and breathe. The boys escaped out the door.

At a Moosic breaker, the boys plotted to teach their mean boss a lesson. Instead of going to work one July morning, they went swimming.

Their boss found them at the swimming hole and ordered them to report to the breaker. As he stood there, two boys rushed him from behind and knocked him into the water, where the other boys were waiting. They dunked the boss again and again. Soon the mine superintendent and another foreman found them. They ordered the boys to stop and get to work.

Suddenly, the boys realized that they were in a position to bargain. The boys refused to return to work unless their mean breaker boss was fired. They shouted back and forth in negotiation until the bosses offered a compromise: they wouldn't fire the mean boss, but he would be transferred to another job, and the boys would be given a new boss. Satisfied, the boys climbed out of the swimming hole and returned to work.

As the boys grew older and moved into other jobs at the colliery, they carried their militant spirit with them. They continued to stick together in their fight for fairer and better living and working conditions. They learned that power was found in numbers.

Gomer Jones and His Crowbar

Many mine workers and their families lived in quiet patch villages like Lattimer, which was tucked into a hillside outside Hazleton, Pennsylvania.

Like most patch villages, Lattimer was laid out according to class. The mine bosses and superintendents lived on the front street, known as Quality Road. They had large, comfortable houses with beautiful lawns. The mine superintendent's office, the company store, a mule barn, and machine repair shop lined the back street. At the end of the back street, a wooden

Like most patch villages, Lattimer was divided ethnically. These children are walking through the Italian section of the village. MG-273 Charles Burg Collection, Pennsylvania State Archives

frame boardinghouse stood. Sixteen immigrant mine workers lived in the boardinghouse.

From the back street, dirt roads led to the mine workers' shanties and shacks. Most were Slavic and Italian immigrants. Their tiny gardens were planted with tomatoes, beans, and other vegetables, as well as hollyhocks, sunflowers, and grapevines. They owned chickens, goats, and pigs. In the distance, two coal breakers rose from the valley north of the village.

Once settled in their new villages, the immigrants were eager to work. Often, they accepted the worst and most dangerous jobs for little pay. Knowing this, coal operators preferred to hire the hardworking immigrants, and Americans became fearful that soon they would lose their jobs to the newcomers. Repeated instances of prejudice and discrimination fueled tension between the Americans and the immigrants.

Although the immigrants shared the same difficult working and living experiences, their diverse backgrounds prevented them from organizing a successful strike. A language barrier created one major problem: as many as twenty-six different languages were spoken in the anthracite region.

One of the most poignant strike attempts occurred on September 10, 1897, a day that became known as the Lattimer massacre. The majority of strikers were men, but teenage boys were also involved in the fight for unionism.

The strike had begun several miles from Lattimer, at the Honey Brook colliery near McAdoo, three weeks earlier. Twenty mule drivers were angry at a new company policy that required them to work two additional hours each day for no additional pay. In protest, the mule drivers formed a picket line to prevent other mine workers from entering the colliery.

When the mine superintendent Gomer Jones saw the picket line, he became incensed. He went into his shed, grabbed a crowbar, and headed for the drivers. He attacked John Bodan, a teenage driver.

But John Bodan managed to grab the crowbar from Jones and began to beat him. Other drivers jumped in. They threw Jones to the ground and pounded him with their fists. One driver grabbed a large rock and held it over Jones's head, ready to dash in his skull. But before the driver could, other bosses saw the fight. They rescued Jones, pulling him to safety.

Jones fired the mule drivers, but they ran to the breaker whistle tower. They blew the whistle, sounding the signal for work to stop. Workers poured from the slag pile, the train cars, and the outbuildings. The breaker machinery ground to a halt, and the breaker boys cheered as they ran home to play. Someone signaled the workers in the mines, and they surfaced, too. By evening, nearly eight hundred mine workers were on strike.

Over the next few days, the story of Gomer Jones and his crowbar spread to other collieries. Soon three thousand workers from six collieries joined the protest. Like the mule drivers, they wanted better working conditions. They

The mule driver was usually a boy in his teens. During the Honey Brook strike, the mule drivers ranged in age from their teens to men in their twenties. Historical Society of Schuykill County

wanted an end to compulsory purchases from the company store and the company butcher. They wanted the privilege of paying for and selecting their own doctor. (The company chose the doctor and deducted his fee from the mine worker's pay, whether or not medical services were rendered.) They also wanted a fifteen percent wage increase and payment for the amount of time they were at the colliery, even when the machinery wasn't working.

The strikers marched to other collieries in the Hazleton region, persuading other mine workers to join them. According to a newspaper reporter, the strikers were armed with clubs, lagging iron, steel rods, and "more effective weapons of argument to convince workers to join the strike." The strikers searched houses, forcing every male occupant, young and old, to join their ranks. In some cases, the strikers didn't care if the men were mine workers: they even forced a Honey Brook schoolteacher to join in their march.

Rumors began to circulate that Gomer Jones was hiding from the strikers, but on August 18, he was arrested for assault. Meanwhile, the strike continued to spread throughout the middle anthracite coalfields. By September 3, more than five thousand mine workers were on strike. The Hazleton area collieries were paralyzed.

The strike had not yet reached Lattimer, where the two coal breakers were still running. The Lattimer mine workers wanted to join the strike, but they wanted to be "called out" so that they would have an excuse. They invited the strikers to Lattimer.

Meanwhile, the county sheriff James Martin was on vacation at the New Jersey seashore. His chief deputy telegraphed him to return home at once. When Martin arrived in Hazleton, he swore in eighty-seven new deputies. He gave each deputy a Winchester rifle, a revolver, and ammunition.

Opportunity, Freedom, and Justice for All

On Friday morning, September 10, 1897, some 250 striking mine workers met in Harwood to begin their march to Lattimer, six miles away. The strikers, mostly Hungarian and Slavic immigrants, dressed in their best clothing. They wore dark trousers, white shirts, and slouch hats. Some wore jackets and ties.

Nineteen-year-old John Eagler found two American flags. He gave them to Joseph Michalko, a strike organizer, and Steve Jurich, a young newlywed. They anticipated a peaceful demonstration: no marcher carried a gun or other weapon.

Jurich and Michalko took their places at the front of the line with the flags. Breaker boys, eager to join the parade, gathered behind them, but they were shooed away by their fathers and other mine workers. It had been decided that the marchers had to be at least fifteen years old. Disappointed, some of the breaker boys went swimming, but several sneaked into the back of the parade.

The command to begin the march was shouted. The mine workers kissed their wives, mothers, and children and waved good-bye.

Along the way, people gathered to watch the parade. The strikers shouted to friends to join them, and soon the number of marchers grew to four hun-

Miners blasted enough coal to fill at least five four-ton coal cars. Wyoming Historical and Geological Society

dred. Seventeen-year-old John Futa joined the parade. As a mine worker he earned seventy-five cents a day, which he gave to his widowed mother. Andrew Meyer also fell into step. It was five days before Andrew's seventeenth birthday. Andrew's family had immigrated from Austria-Hungary to escape ethnic persecution.

As the afternoon wore on, the sun grew hot. The marchers removed their jackets and slung them over their shoulders. They wiped their faces and necks with handkerchiefs.

The men and boys were convinced they had the right to protest for better living and working conditions. In the mines, accidents, injury, and even death were common. On the average, nearly one mine worker was killed each day

The mule driver sat on the car bumper, using only his voice to guide the mule. Mules knew how many cars they had to pull and how many chambers they had to visit. Stubborn mules refused to do additional work. Pennsylvania Historical and Museum Commission, Anthracite Museum Complex

from a roof fall, explosion, or other accident. Sometimes the men worked knee-deep in water or on their hands and knees in chambers too low to stand. They had to buy their own supplies—tools, oil, blasting powder, wooden props, and blacksmithing—and pay their own helpers. Each of their coal cars had to be "topped," or heaped, with extra coal or else they weren't paid. Even though a topped coal car weighed four tons, the miner was paid only for two or three tons of coal. The rest, the company claimed, was rubble.

The younger boys had grievances, too. "Nippers," or door tenders, sat in the dark on a pine bench all day long, listening for the rumble of approaching mine cars. When they heard the cars, they had to open the doors so the cars could pass through. There would be serious trouble if they fell asleep. Spraggers had even more dangerous jobs. They had to control the speed of the rolling mine cars by jabbing wooden sprags into the wheels. Some spraggers lost fingers, hands, or legs in accidents. Mule drivers often had nasty or stubborn mules that refused to work by lying down on the job.

Yet, despite their grievances, the immigrant strikers on their way to Lattimer were filled with patriotic loyalty for their new homeland. This was America—land of opportunity, freedom, and justice for all. As the American flags fluttered at the front of the parade, the marchers were convinced that their lives would improve in their new country.

"We'll Give You Hell, Not Water"

Meanwhile, someone alerted Sheriff James Martin that the strikers were headed for Lattimer. He and his deputies arrived in Lattimer by trolley, ahead of the strikers. He ordered his men to station themselves along the single road that led into the village. He gave the deputies final instructions for their rifles.

When Lattimer residents saw the deputies and their guns, they became alarmed. Many retreated into their homes and watched anxiously from their windows. Worried mothers ran to the schoolhouse and took their children home. The two teachers dismissed the rest of the students and stood in the schoolhouse doorway. They watched the sheriff, the deputies, and the road to Lattimer.

At three-thirty, a cloud of dust rose over the hill. Soon the procession of men and boys became visible. Steve Jurich, John Eagler, Joseph Michalko, and the others saw the sheriff and the line of deputies, but they continued. They marched past the deputies until they reached Sheriff Martin.

The sheriff ordered them to disperse. "This is contrary to the law and you are creating a disturbance," he told Steve Jurich and the others. "You must go back. I won't let you go on to the colliery."

Someone behind Steve yelled, "Go on," and the marchers pressed forward.

Nearly four hundred striking men and teenage boys marched six miles from Harwood to Lattimer. Unarmed, they believed the American flag would show their peaceful intent. MG-273 Charles Burg Collection, Pennsylvania State Archives

What happened next is unclear. Some people say the sheriff fell down; others say he was pushed. Some say the sheriff yelled "Fire!" and ordered his deputies to shoot. Others say a deputy yelled "Fire!"

But the events of the following three minutes are clearly documented. According to a newspaper reporter, "The guns were suddenly raised and just as quickly the deadly fire began."

A full volley of shots rang out. The first bullets tore open Steve Jurich's head. He fell, crying in Slovak to God, *"O Joj! Joj! Joj!"* and then he died. Bullets shattered Andrew Meyer's knees. His right leg would later be amputated. John Futa was shot dead.

From the schoolhouse, the teachers watched in horror. At first one teacher thought the deputies were firing blanks, but then she saw that some of the fallen men didn't get up. Witnesses said the deputies ran after some of the fleeing men to get better shots. Some strikers were shot in the back as they ran for cover. "We ran," said Martin Rosko, who was shot in the arm, "but they kept on shooting while we ran." Other strikers threw themselves down, praying the bullets would pass over them. There was nowhere to hide.

Finally, the shooting stopped. All around, wounded and dying men cried and groaned and shrieked in pain. Some cried for water. When the deputies heard the cries, they yelled back, "We'll give you hell, not water, hunkies."

The teachers began to administer help until several doctors arrived. The schoolhouse was turned into a hospital.

The massacre left nineteen dead and at least thirty-two wounded. Of the dead and wounded, several were teenage boys. As the deputies rode out of Lattimer on the trolley, witnesses said the deputies were laughing and joking about how many men they had killed.

Sheriff James Martin and his deputies went on trial that fall. Their attorney argued that the sheriff and deputies acted courageously and prevented a civil war from breaking out in the region between immigrants and native-born Americans. The jury returned a verdict of "not guilty."

The deputies celebrated their victory at the Old Hazle Brewery. From then on, the Hazle beer became known as "Deputies' Beer," and people boycotted it. Within six months, the brewery went bankrupt.

A mob also attacked Gomer Jones's house. They broke doors, smashed windows, and destroyed everything in sight. A newspaper editorial said, "Gomer has learned a lesson. He has been taught a man is a man even if he is a Hungarian."

"A Johnny Mitchell Man"

After the Lattimer massacre, the anthracite mine workers knew that they had to unite. The entire anthracite region had to strike together. To do so, they needed a leader.

John Mitchell was a tireless young labor leader. Orphaned at the age of six, young John was raised by a stern stepmother. He left home when he was ten and worked at a variety of jobs. At twelve, he began to work in the bituminous coal mines in Illinois and rose quickly from nipper to miner's helper. At thirteen, he helped rescue miners after a disaster.

John's experiences led him to realize that the mine workers needed

John Mitchell rose from mine worker to president of the United Mine Workers. Library of Congress

a union. When he was eighteen, he joined the United Mine Workers. Over the next ten years, he proved himself to be a successful leader as he worked to organize the bituminous miners in Illinois, Indiana, Ohio, and western Pennsylvania.

By 1899, twenty-nine-year-old John Mitchell was named president of the United Mine Workers. With gains already won in the bituminous coalfields, he turned his attention to the anthracite region in eastern Pennsylvania.

Mitchell knew it wouldn't be easy to organize such a diverse group of workers, but by 1900, he won the anthracite mine workers' trust and respect. His good looks and youthful appearance earned him the names "Boy President" and "Old Young Man." He usually dressed like a member of the clergy, in a long black coat, black tie, and high white collar. To the mine workers, he seemed modest but confident, dignified, and honest.

For the boys, the greatest honor was to be a "union man" or "Johnny Mitchell man." Like their fathers, the boys joined the United Mine Workers and soon comprised twenty percent of the membership. At the union meetings, the young delegates numbered enough to sway the votes. They often held the balance of power when policy was being decided.

As junior union members, the boys met secretly each week and paid monthly dues. Only members who knew the password were admitted to the meetings. At every meeting, the breaker boys listened intently to the older boys.

The boys knew they needed the support of every worker, and they pressured the nonunion workers to join. Mule drivers were especially effective: they refused to deliver empty coal cars to nonunion workers. The boys stuck together. If they thought one of their junior members was treated unfairly, they staged a strike.

Loyalty spread to the backyards, alleys, churches, and schools. At home, children refused to play with other children whose fathers didn't belong to the union. One small boy, rejected by the other children because his father was nonunion, pleaded, "I'll be a Johnny Mitchell man, only let me play."

After a year of organizing, the people of the anthracite coal region felt powerful enough to force the coal companies to listen to them. The mine workers drew up a list of their grievances: they wanted a wage increase, different weighing procedures for the coal, an eight-hour day, and an end to job favoritism. In August 1900, they asked John Mitchell to call a general strike.

At first Mitchell hesitated. He considered a strike to be a last resort. But when the mine owners refused to negotiate, Mitchell called a general anthracite strike on September 17, 1900. The timing of the strike was critical: soon Americans would need anthracite to heat their homes during the winter months. Furthermore, the strike would affect hundreds of other industries fueled by anthracite. Surely, the strikers thought, these factors would force the coal companies to listen to their grievances.

Eighty thousand mine workers stopped work. The union leaders were

Mothers worried about the bad habits that their sons acquired at work, namely swearing, smoking, and chewing tobacco. Though the boys handed their pay envelopes to their mothers, they usually "knocked down" their wages, keeping a few nickels for themselves to buy candy or, in this case, tobacco. Library of Congress

"Mother" Mary Harris Jones organized mine workers by marching from colliery to colliery, despite threats by coal operators to use force to stop her. Historical Society of Schuylkill County

gleeful. Large groups of workers marched from colliery to colliery in order to shut them down. Within a week, more than 125,000 men and boys were on strike.

Seventy-year-old Mary Harris Jones, a longtime labor agitator known to the miners as Mother Jones, appeared in the region. With her white hair, she looked more like a grandmother than a labor leader, but her organizing efforts had earned her the name "Miner's Angel."

Mother Jones dressed in a long black shirtwaist dress and flowered hat. Wielding an umbrella, she marched from colliery to colliery, calling the mine workers to turn out. Children paraded behind her. She was so effective that the police threatened to use force to stop her. Mitchell intervened and convinced Mother Jones to cut back.

When John Mitchell arrived in the anthracite region, the breaker boys followed his horse-drawn carriage. Library of Congress

By early October, nearly every colliery in the anthracite region was idle. The strike made newspaper headlines across the nation. Though people all over the country worried about fuel during the approaching winter months, many were sympathetic toward the mine workers. The coal companies were pressured into meeting with union leaders.

The forty-three-day strike ended on October 29, 1900, when the mine workers accepted a wage increase. Throughout the anthracite region, John Mitchell was hailed as a hero. The mine workers voted to make October 29 "Mitchell Day."

But the battle wasn't won yet. The United Mine Workers, bolstered by their partial success, spent over a year organizing another strike. In 1902 the mine workers went on strike again. This time, 140,000 mine workers and their families united. They were determined to win, no matter what the consequences.

They waved flags, sang ballads, hung banners, and marched in parades. "There were daylight parades, before-breakfast parades, and parades after midnight," said one man. A bugle and drum corps led the marchers, who sang, cheered, and laughed as loudly as they could. They often stopped at the homes of scabs to serenade them.

The community united, too. Landlords wouldn't rent rooms to strikebreakers, and hotels and restaurants wouldn't serve them. No barber would shave a strikebreaker. In some church parishes, entire classes and choirs disappeared if their Sunday school teachers and choirmasters weren't union sympathizers.

The strikers and their families looked for other ways to earn money. They picked huckleberries that grew in abundance on the mountains. They cultivated their gardens, chickens, and livestock. They trimmed living expenses as much as possible, which affected many other businesses throughout the region. When the militia set up camp, the children sold small carvings made of coal to the soldiers and panhandled for money.

Children sneaked past guards and "No Trespassing" signs to scavenge coal from the culm banks, the large piles of refuse from the breaker. They peddled bags of coal in nearby towns.

When police caught the children, they smashed their baskets and wagons. One seven-year-old girl explained why the culm banks were guarded so carefully: "All the people 'round here is striking. So of course the company wants them to starve. If they can't get coal to cook their food with, they will starve faster."

A strike also meant the children had plenty of time to attend school. The children carried their union loyalty to class. Children of mine workers staged a school walkout when they discovered that the father of one of their teachers was a scab. The students demanded that their teacher be fired.

School strikes didn't usually last long because the leaders were quickly expelled. But many adults agreed that "they couldn't stand for having their children learning in the same room with a nonunion child."

During the strike, women and children picked coal from the culm banks. Wyoming Historical and Geological Society

The 1902 strike brought much hardship to the anthracite region. Not everyone sympathized with the strikers, especially the coal operators who wanted to continue to make huge profits and those who didn't want to pay higher prices for coal.

Some coal operators evicted the mine workers and their families from their company-owned housing. Many mine workers were hungry, penniless,

During the 1902 strike, mine operator John Markle evicted his workers from their company-owned homes. Pennsylvania Historical and Museum Commission, Bureau of Historic Sites and Museums, Anthracite Museum Complex

homeless, and scared. Thirty thousand workers fled to other parts of the country, hoping to find other work. Fifteen thousand immigrants went back to their homelands. In many families, the oldest children ran away, knowing that extra mouths to feed were a burden. Hundreds of these boys and girls hopped freight trains and headed for big cities such as New York and Philadelphia.

To the strikers, the most grievous crime of all was to be a scab. As the strike wore on, some families were divided forever when some members decided to cross a picket line and continue to work. They felt betrayed by their fellow workers who turned scab and by the strikebreakers who were brought in to work from outside the region. The striking mine workers often assaulted the scabs and strikebreakers by dunking them in creeks and rivers and throwing

Striking men and boys chased scabs. If the scabs were caught, they were beaten up or dunked in creeks. Everybody's Magazine, Vol. 7, September 1902

stones at them. Strikers dug graves in the yards of strikebreakers and inscribed the strikebreakers' names on tombstones as warnings. Strikers sent threatening letters to the strikebreakers' families. They even blew up the porches of scab workers with dynamite.

For protection, the coal companies hired additional police and even brought in state troops. Soldiers escorted the scabs and strikebreakers to and from work. Mother Jones returned to the region. She made speeches, calling the coal operators "sewer rats" and organizing labor marches of children.

State troops were sent in to guard the colliery property and to maintain law and order. Here the troops are stationed in front of the breaker. Wyoming Historical and Geological Society

The strike affected the entire country. Throughout the nation, people feared a severe coal shortage during the winter months. The strike also had a deep impact on the anthracite region as the wages of the mine workers disappeared from the local economy. Merchants, retailers, and wholesalers lost huge amounts of business.

"A Harrowing Tale"

Finally, President Theodore Roosevelt intervened and demanded that the coal operators arbitrate with the mine workers. The operators refused at first, but they changed their minds when Roosevelt threatened to confiscate their properties. He appointed an Anthracite Commission to study the miners' grievances. The strike ended October 23, 1902. It had lasted 165 days.

The attorney Clarence Darrow represented the mine workers at the arbitration hearings. Throughout the testimony, children like ten-year-old Andrew Chippie took the stand along with the adults. In 1901, Andrew's father was killed in the mines as a result of a roof fall. Andrew's widowed mother took in boarders and tried to make ends meet so that her children could stay in school.

Soon Andrew, the oldest of the four children, had to quit school to work in the breaker. Andrew never received one cent for his work. When his father died, he owed one hundred dollars to the company store. The coal company applied all of Andrew's earnings toward his father's debt.

The newspapers called it a "harrowing tale," more distressing than the stories of injured miners. Headlines said, "Company Took Boy's Money." One newspaper reporter claimed: "The entire commission and all those that heard the story of little Andrew Chippie were moved to compassion for the little lad and his mother."

After months of testimony, the Anthracite Commission made its decision: it awarded the mine workers a pay increase and an eight-hour day for certain types of mine work. Weighing men would now be paid by the miners, in the hopes of eliminating unfair dockages. As John Mitchell and others long hoped, the commission also criticized the employment of children under fourteen.

Would success have been possible without the youthful militancy of the children? Their testimony and union allegiance increased public awareness of the problems of child labor. It would still take years to eradicate child labor in the anthracite mines, but lawmakers would continue to pass stronger and more effective legislation.

Meanwhile, the children would continue the fight for labor reform and better living conditions.

CHAPTER FIVE

"WE ASK YOU, MR. PRESIDENT"

Mother Jones and Her Industrial Army Philadelphia (1903)

Eleven-year-old Gus Rangnow worked in a Kensington hosiery factory, where he packed stockings, hour after hour, for eleven hours each day. He worked nearly that long on Saturdays. The long days and lack of sleep showed in his face, which a reporter described as the face of an old person.

Eddie Dunphy was twelve. For eleven hours each day, he sat on a high stool and handed thread to the worker next to him. Dangerous

Striking Kensington mill children wanted to work fifty-five hours each week instead of sixty. Corbis-Bettman

machinery clanked and whirled around him. He knew to be careful. He had seen the crushed hands and missing fingers of the boys and girls.

Ten-year-old James Ashworth walked all day, carrying bundles of yarn from one department to the next. The bundles weighed seventy-five pounds, too much for any child whose bones were still growing. Already, James's stooped back and shoulders showed signs of deformity: he looked like an old man.

Gus, Eddie, and James lived and worked in Kensington, Pennsylvania, a mill district outside Philadelphia. In 1903, most Kensington families found work at the mills, where everything from coats to dresses to shirts to stockings to carpets were produced. As in other mills and factories throughout the country, Kensington children doffed bobbins, tended spinning looms and spindles, cleaned machinery, swept floors, and performed countless other jobs.

The mill workers wanted their weekly hours reduced from sixty to fifty-five. For sixteen thousand mill children like Gus, James, and Eddie, five fewer work hours meant more time to play or attend night school. According to one reformer, many working children could barely read or even spell their own names.

In most labor struggles for a shorter workweek, the workers demanded that their hours be reduced and their wages remain the same. Although wages were already low, the Kensington workers agreed to accept reduced wages in return for a shorter workweek. In April 1903, the Kensington workers sent a delegation to approach the mill owners. The delegation requested that the workweek be reduced by five hours.

The mill owners refused, even though it is unlikely that their profits would have been affected. New machinery made it possible for workers to produce as much in fifty-five hours as they did in sixty. Because most workers were paid by the piece, production mattered, not the number of hours.

So why did the owners refuse? They claimed that the working conditions in their factories were already better than the workers deserved. They called the workers' grievances and threats of a strike unfair and unjust.

The mill owners met at the Manufacturers' Club in Philadelphia and formed their own association. They promised that they wouldn't give in to the workers' demands. To ensure that each mill owner remained resolute, the association developed a forfeit plan. Each owner contributed a substantial amount of money to a forfeit pool: the amount of the forfeit depended upon the size of the factory and the amount of equipment it had. In the event

By 1900, Mother Jones was a well-known labor agitator, famous for her wit, sharp tongue, and organizing ability. The Archives of Labor and Urban Affairs, Wayne State University

of a strike, any mill owner who gave in to the workers' demands would lose his forfeited money.

The workers announced a strike for Monday morning, June 1, 1903. On that day, six hundred mills opened as usual. The bosses and owners waited for the stream of children, women, and men to come through the doors. But most of the workers never came. Nearly one hundred thousand workers, including sixteen thousand children, stayed home. The Kensington mill strike of 1903 had begun.

"I've Got Stock in These Little Children"
News of the Kensington strike traveled to West Virginia, where "Mother" Mary Harris Jones was working to organize the bituminous coal mine workers. As soon as she heard about the Kensington mill children, she packed a bag and headed for Pennsylvania.

Mother Jones arrived in Philadelphia on June 14. By then, the Kensington strike was in its third week, and the strikers were growing anxious. A few small mill owners had conceded, but the larger mill owners wouldn't budge. They didn't seem concerned either: they simply canceled work orders, sat back, and waited for the strikers to give up. They knew that their impoverished workers couldn't hold out forever.

Mother Jones headed straight for union headquarters, where she met some of the striking children. She was horrified. The children seemed incredibly small and skinny for their ages. Some had missing fingers and hands. Their shoulders were rounded from bending over machinery for so many hours each day. Their backs were stooped from carrying heavy bundles.

Mother Jones sought out the local newspaper reporters. "Why don't you publish this and make comment on it?" she asked them.

Many reporters knew the facts on child labor. In 1903, more children worked in industries in Pennsylvania than in any other state. State law prohibited children under twelve from working, but loopholes and poor enforcement created weak child labor laws, allowing many children to work illegally. In fact, reformers claimed, Pennsylvania had the weakest child labor legislation. Since Pennsylvania had the greatest number of industries that profited from child labor, it seemed that no state had greater need for reform.

But the reporters told Mother Jones that they didn't dare to publish the facts on Pennsylvania's child labor. The mill owners owned stock in the newspapers. The editors wouldn't publish stories that criticized the stockholders. They feared that they would lose their jobs.

This infuriated Mother Jones. "Well, I've got stock in these little children," she said. "I'll arrange a little publicity." She sent telegraphs to the New York papers. She told them about the striking children and asked them to send down reporters to cover a mass meeting.

The New York City reporters accepted her invitation. In Philadelphia, on June 17, the reporters gathered in Independence Park, along with Mother Jones and more than six thousand children, some maimed or injured from their work.

In her usual black shirtwaist and flowered hat, Mother Jones stood with the children, just as she had done during the 1900 and 1902 anthracite coal mining strikes. She led the striking children out of the park, past the Liberty Bell, through the business district, and past the newspaper offices. More than likely, she wanted to show all of Philadelphia the story that their reporters and publishers didn't have the guts to print.

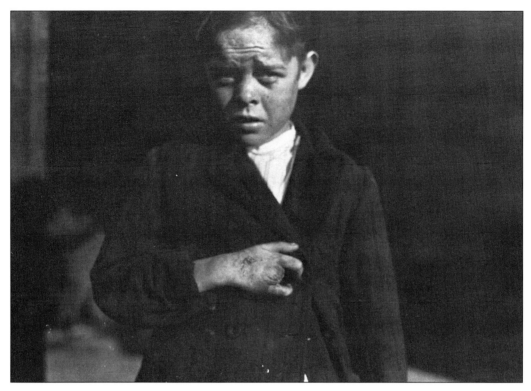

Many mill children lost fingers working with the dangerous machinery.
Photography Collection, University of Maryland Baltimore County

The procession of children stopped in front of city hall, filling the public square and jamming the streets. City officials stood in the courthouse windows and watched the crowd below.

Mother Jones lifted two small boys onto a table and showed what machinery had done to their hands and fingers. She held up the smallest workers, so that the city officials could see them. She pointed to the puny arms and legs and sunken chest of each child.

Then she stood on the platform and began to speak. Famous for her sharp tongue and quick wit, she scolded the city's rich citizens and shamed the well-to-do. "Philadelphia's mansions [are] built on the broken bones, the quivering hearts, and drooping heads of these children," she told the crowd.

The publicity worked for a short while. New York City reporters wrote

The girls are lacing skeins of silk on a reeling machine. Pennsylvania Historical and Museum Commission, Anthracite Museum Complex

about the demonstration and quoted her in their stories. For several days, wherever people read the newspapers, people were talking about child labor.

Yet the mill owners and city officials remained silent, waiting for the public's interest to wane. It did. After several days, the public's attention turned to other issues.

But if the mill owners thought that Mother Jones would give up, they were wrong. Her fierce determination and crustiness had earned her the reputation as the "most dangerous woman in America."

"The Most Dangerous Woman in America"

In 1903, Mother Jones claimed to be seventy-three. More than thirty years earlier, a yellow fever epidemic had killed her husband and children in Tennessee. "One by one, my four little children sickened and died," she wrote in her autobiography. "I washed their little bodies and got them ready for burial. My husband caught the fever and died. I sat alone through nights of grief. . . . All day long, all night long, I heard the grating of the wheels of the death cart."

The yellow fever mostly struck the poor and the working class, who couldn't afford to escape the diseased city, as the wealthy could. Unable to afford nurses, doctors, and medicine, the poor simply suffered and died. They were buried at night, quietly and without ceremony.

Left alone, Mother Jones moved to Chicago. To earn a living, she opened a dressmaking shop. There, once again, she became haunted by the contrast between the wealthy and the poor. As she sat in her shop, sewing fine clothes for the wealthy, she looked out her window and saw "the poor, shivering wretches, jobless and hungry" who could not afford food, clothing, and a place to sleep.

In 1871, the Chicago fire destroyed her dressmaking shop. After the disaster, she opened a new shop next door to the office of the Knights of Labor. At night, she attended their rallies and listened as they preached the importance of sacrifice for the cause of labor.

During the railroad strike of 1877, she witnessed strikers shot down by the

Mother Jones leads a parade of workers. Her demonstrations often included children. The Archives of Labor and Urban Affairs, Wayne State University

militia. She saw how unfairly the strikers were treated. "The strikers were charged with the crimes of arson and rioting," she said, "although it was common knowledge that it was not they who instigated the fire. . . . Then and there I learned . . . that labor must bear the cross for others' sins."

She devoted the rest of her life to the cause of labor. Until she was nearly one hundred years old, Mother Jones went wherever the need was greatest. She sneaked across militia lines, defied death threats, and incurred the wrath of judges, who sent her to jail. She angered governors, presidents, and factory, mill, and mine operators as she spoke out against abusive work conditions. She organized workers into unions and rallied men, women, and children. With Mother Jones as their leader, groups of women and girls shamed scabs into joining the union.

After several years of organizing mine workers, she began to hear stories about the cotton mills. In 1896, she decided to investigate. She applied for a job in an Alabama cotton mill. The manager told her she couldn't have a job unless she had a family who could also work. Mother Jones lied and said that she had six children who also needed work.

The manager hired her immediately. "He was so enthusiastic," said Mother Jones, "that he went with me to find a house to rent." The house was a two-story plank shanty with broken windows, sagging door, and a cracked roof.

Mother Jones found working conditions even more gruesome than she had imagined. At five-thirty each morning, she saw long lines of children going to work at the mills. She saw children who fell asleep at lunch, too tired to eat their cornbread and fat pork, and lint-covered babies, asleep on pillows as their mothers worked. She heard their coughs and rattles, sure signs of pneumonia or consumption caused by lint-filled lungs. She saw hands crushed by machinery and fingers snapped off, shoulders stooped and rounded from work. She saw an eleven-year-old girl who died when her hair became caught in the machinery. The girl's scalp had been torn from her head.

Mother Jones also heard Sunday sermons, when the ministers preached that mill owners were inspired to build their mills so "[God's] little ones [might] work that they might develop into industrious, patriotic citizens." Although she was outraged at the hypocrisy of the system, she never organized the women who worked in the factories and mills. She concentrated most of her effort in the coal mining regions.

The Crusade Begins

In Philadelphia, as the nation celebrated the Fourth of July, Mother Jones became inspired by the crowds that flocked to see the Liberty Bell in Independence Park. The striking children, she decided, had much in common with the Liberty Bell. Like the patriots during the American Revolution, the children were also fighting for freedom from oppression. They were fighting for the right to go to school, the right to play, the right to childhood.

Suddenly, it dawned on her. If a short march through the streets of Philadelphia could get people talking about child labor, then a longer march might spur them beyond words and into action. She began to plan a crusade of children; she envisioned an army of striking children wending their way from Philadelphia to New York City, 125 miles away.

Along the route, she planned to hold rallies and demonstrations and give speeches denouncing the evils of child labor and the manufacturers who employed children. In New York City, she hoped that their presence would shame the Wall Street businessmen who owned stock in the very mills and factories that exploited the children and their families.

She also knew that President Theodore Roosevelt and his family were spending the summer at Oyster Bay on Long Island. She wanted the president to see her army of children. "Let him see these mill children," she said, "and compare with his own little ones at Oyster Bay."

She hoped her crusade would call national attention to the plight of child workers and force President Theodore Roosevelt and the American voters to support federal legislation to restrict and regulate child labor.

On July 7, Mother Jones met with union officials and the parents of striking children. She explained the crusade and asked the parents for permission to take their children on her march. Many parents agreed.

Excited, Gus Rangnow, James Ashworth, Eddie Dunphy, and other children ran home. They packed knives, forks, spoons, tin cups and plates, and clothing in their knapsacks. Mother Jones had hoped to enlist four hundred children and their parents, about eight hundred in all, but she settled for less than half that amount. Although numbers vary in newspaper accounts, an estimated three hundred children, women, and men joined the industrial army. One newspaper, the Philadelphia *North American,* even sent a reporter along. Jack Lopez would write a first-hand account of the crusade.

Mother Jones selected leaders from the striking men: John Donnelly, John Sweeney, and Edward Hinklesmith. Donnelly and Sweeney would ride bicycles ahead of the army to scout out camps. Hinklesmith obtained eight

Mother Jones was appalled at the hypocrisy of the southern mill system, which mill owners and ministers alike claimed would bring great wealth to the south. In this picture, a young boy is tending a spinning machine in a southern mill.
Photography Collection, University of Maryland Baltimore County

large wagons to carry the food and other supplies. Storekeepers donated canned goods and bread. Arrangements were made to send money and food donations ahead to planned bases.

By one o'clock on July 7, the children stood in line, holding banners and placards and waving flags. Fifes played, drums rolled, and the order was called to move out. The wagons lurched forward. The mill children's crusade had begun.

"My Poor Boys and Girls"

As the first afternoon wore on, many marchers couldn't keep up in the unbearable heat. They fell from the ranks, straggled behind, and returned home.

But Mother Jones pressed on, sometimes walking, sometimes riding, to reach the towns ahead of the crusaders. Once there, she sought out places for them to eat and sleep and meeting halls from which she could speak.

By July 10, three days after the march had begun, some crusaders became disgusted when they saw that Mother Jones slept in hotels and rode in cars or on trains. "It's all right for Mother Jones," one man grumbled. "She sleeps in a hotel. I would rather work sixty hours a week than endure this torture." He went home.

The poor food upset John Donnelly, who tried to depose Mother Jones and take over the crusade. When that failed, he and several other men went home.

Mother Jones scolded her army and told the rest of the malcontents to go home. Many did, one hundred in all. However, nearly that many fresh recruits arrived from Philadelphia.

Some reporters chided Mother Jones, calling the march too strenuous for the children, but she disagreed. She maintained that the children enjoyed the freedom from their work and their bosses, from the drudgery of long hours and noisy machinery. Was the march any harder than their work?

Reporter Jack Lopez agreed with Mother Jones, noting: "The marchers are sunburned and look in better health than when they left Philadelphia. The little boys' faces have filled out, and their eyes have brightened with the week of out-of-door life in the pure air."

In addition to meager food rations, they also endured rainstorms. In the midst of a driving rainstorm outside Princeton, New Jersey, Mother Jones walked nearly a mile to find shelter for the group. Drenched to the skin, she arrived at the door of former President Grover Cleveland's mansion. A caretaker answered the door and told her that Cleveland and his family were on vacation.

Mother Jones described her children's army to the caretaker and told him

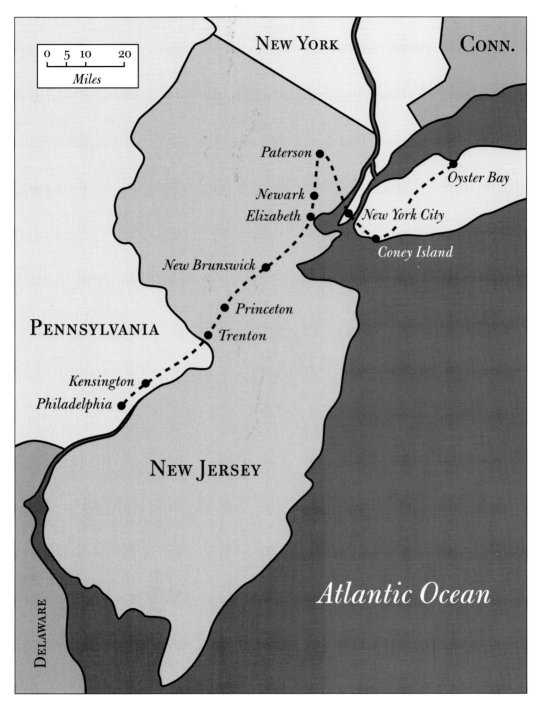

Mother Jones planned a 125-mile "Children's Crusade" through parts of
Pennsylvania, New Jersey, and New York.

that it was Cleveland's duty to give them shelter. The caretaker offered to let them sleep in the barn if they promised to stay off the front lawn.

Mother Jones went back through the rain to find her army waiting at the railroad station. When they heard the good news, they cheered and clapped. But before they could leave the station, the caretaker, "wild-eyed and disheveled," rushed in. "It was a mistake," he told them. "I withdraw my invitation. It would ruin me." The caretaker had changed his mind after speaking to one of Cleveland's friends.

Disappointed, Mother Jones and her army boarded the next train, headed for New Brunswick. Jack Lopez summarized how the army felt: "Grover Cleveland's reputation had dropped a peg, and he hundreds of miles away."

"The Wail of the Children"

When the army reached New Brunswick, a local hotel manager allowed the crusaders to sleep in a barn near a picnic grove. Mother Jones gave the army a day off to mend their clothing. The children bathed in brooks and rivers, played in the grassy fields, ate potatoes and vegetable soup, and slept. They went fishing and feasted on catfish. With her own money, Mother Jones bought shoes for some of the crusaders.

Two days later, they arrived in Elizabeth. Mother Jones wrote a letter to President Roosevelt, explaining that the Kensington workers were striking for a fifty-five-hour workweek and asking to see him. The letter was mailed to the president and published in several newspapers.

In her next speech, Mother Jones verbally attacked the young college men attending nearby Princeton University. "They are wasting their money on an education which will do them no good," she told the crowds. "Go into the mills of Philadelphia and see the children risking their lives when they ought to be in school." Mother Jones wasn't against education. All her life, she said, she encouraged people to read and to learn. But she wanted them to use their knowledge to help those less fortunate. She expected no less from the students and professors at ivy-covered colleges and universities like Princeton.

President Theodore Roosevelt and his family spent their summers at Oyster Bay, Long Island, New York. Library of Congress

When a Princeton professor invited Mother Jones to speak to his class, she took ten-year-old James Ashworth along. "Here," she told the class as she pointed to James, "is a textbook on economics. He gets three dollars a week and his sister, who is fourteen, six dollars. They work in a carpet factory ten hours a day while the children of the rich are getting their higher education."

The army continued to dwindle as crusaders dropped out. Some newspaper reporters claimed that Mother Jones was at her wits' end trying to keep her crusade together. They also wrote that President Roosevelt had no official information about her intent to see him. A presidential spokesman said that Roosevelt would not meet with Mother Jones without advance arrangements.

Mother Jones reminded reporters that she had written and mailed President Roosevelt a letter.

Rumors began to circulate that secret service agents tailed Mother Jones and her dwindling army. She claimed that agents had visited her and warned her to call off the march. Yet she remained undaunted. "If the president refuses to see the children," she said, "I will stir up such a sentiment among the workers that he cannot again be president."

On July 19, Mother Jones assured a crowd in Paterson, New Jersey: "I am going to complete my journey to Oyster Bay with my army to see the president. The newspapers say he will not see me. I am going to find out if he is the president of the capitalists only, or whether he is the president of the workingmen, too."

A group of striking Kensington mill children posed before the march began.
Comrade, Fall 1903

Throughout the march, Mother Jones was reminded constantly of the contrasting lifestyles between the wealthy and the poor. In parks, she saw neatly dressed children who didn't have to work. They had time to have egg races and skip rope. She remarked how glad she was that they had the opportunity to play and go to school.

When Mother Jones and her crusaders finally reached New York City on July 23, the police commissioner denied her a parade permit because she and her marchers weren't city residents. She went over his head to Mayor Low. "These are the little citizens of the nation and they produce the nation's wealth," she told the mayor. He granted her the parade permit. He also assigned six hundred policemen from eleven police stations to watch over the march.

At eight o'clock that evening, an army band consisting of two fifes and two drums assembled on Fourth Avenue. The children carried signs that read

On the march, Mother Jones often looked after the children herself. Here she is combing a young crusader's hair.

Philadelphia *North American*, July 13, 1903

"Fifty-five Hours or Nothing," "Give Us More Schools," and "Prosperity: Where's Our Share?"

A crowd of young people from the East Side followed the army through the streets. They shouted and cheered, creating as much noise as a full regiment. At the end of the parade, an exhausted Mother Jones spoke for a short time about the child slavery that was taking place in mills and factories throughout the country. She assured the crowd that she intended to reach Oyster Bay and that, once there, she hoped that the president would see her. "I will take only three little boys with me," she said. "If he refuses to see the boys, why, I will not see him, that's certain."

Mother Jones and the children spent two days at Coney Island. For the first time in their lives, the mill children saw and did what wealthy children took for granted. They enjoyed an animal show of trained lions, monkeys, and even an elephant.

There, Mother Jones spoke to a gathered crowd. At one point she put the children in the empty cages left on stage from the animal show. The children clung to the bars as she told the crowd: "We want President Roosevelt to hear the wail of the children who never have a chance to go to school but work eleven and twelve hours a day in the textile mills of Pennsylvania; who weave the carpets that he and you walk upon, and the lace curtains in your windows, and the clothes of the people."

Along the march, children and other army members collected donations. When Mother Jones discovered that unauthorized people were collecting money for themselves, she created identification cards. Philadelphia North American, July 11, 1903

"Teddy Was Scared of Me"

Meanwhile, the officials at Oyster Bay were seething. Mother Jones was still insisting on a visit with the president. Didn't she know that a person couldn't just demand an audience with the president, not even someone like Mother Jones?

One newspaper headline touted the admonishment: "'Mother' Mustn't 'Storm' President." Others told how secret service men, police, and detectives "kept a sharp lookout" and wary eye on Mother Jones and her now two dozen ragged crusaders.

To prevent her from reaching Oyster Bay on foot, the police created roadblocks. Secret service men patrolled the trains, looking for Mother Jones and her band of children. They looked for children dressed in rags and carrying signs and banners. But they didn't find them. They watched and listened for fifes, drums, and banners, but they didn't find any. Had Mother Jones changed her mind?

On July 28, nobody paid much attention to the three well-dressed young boys who sat quietly with a middle-aged man on a train headed for Long Island. When the train arrived, the travelers got off and disappeared along one of the back streets.

Nobody paid much attention to the later arrival of a sweet-faced, white-haired woman, dressed impeccably in a starched black shirtwaist. She walked from the station into town and climbed into a closed carriage.

The travelers reached the gates outside President Roosevelt's home in

Mother Jones knew that federal laws were necessary to keep children from working. Library of Congress

Oyster Bay without incident. They introduced themselves: Mother Jones, John Sweeney, Gus Rangnow, Eddie Dunphy, and James Ashworth.

The secret service ushered them through the gates and into a private room. After a few minutes, they were joined by B. F. Barnes, the president's private secretary.

Mother Jones told Mr. Barnes that she wanted President Roosevelt to see the children who worked in the factories and mills. Surely, after hearing their stories, he would see the need for child labor reform.

Mr. Barnes told her that she would have to write a letter. She couldn't just drop in on the president.

"But we have already written two letters," said Mother Jones. "We cannot spend the time waiting on the whim of you folks. Either allow us the interview or tell us we will not get it."

"You must understand that Mr. Roosevelt is here to rest," said Mr. Barnes. "He cannot be bothered by matters which can be settled by us. If we allowed everyone to see him, he would have no time for himself."

The secretary also told her that President Roosevelt had no authority in these matters. Child labor was the business of the states, not the federal government. It was up to each state to regulate child labor. Put your concerns in writing, he told Mother Jones again.

Mother Jones insisted: "Then I am to take it that I am to return to Philadelphia and tell 125,000 textile workers that I cannot get an interview without all this red tape?"

"You can do as you will," said Mr. Barnes. "Perhaps that will be better for all of us." It was a bitter disappointment for Mother Jones and the children. After marching more than 125 miles, they had been turned down by the one man who she believed could have made a difference: the president of the United States.

She never forgave Theodore Roosevelt. Years later, she called him a "monkey chaser," referring to his safari hunting expeditions in Africa. She said: "That fellow Roosevelt had secret service men from his palace at Oyster Bay, all the way to New York, to watch an old gray-headed woman. . . . Teddy was scared of me."

She didn't forgive his private secretary either. "[Barnes] was afraid I would dynamite him," she said. "He has died since in Washington. I was glad when I heard of it."

Retreat was uncharacteristic of Mother Jones, but what more could she do? She had spent twenty-two days on the road and had succeeded in getting national attention for working children. "Our march had done its work," she later wrote.

Mother Mary Harris Jones and her handful of mill children quietly retreated to Philadelphia. On August 17, the Kensington workers returned to the mills, defeated. The mill owners won because the hungry strikers had run out of money.

When the children returned to Kensington, they went back to sixty-hour workweeks. Library of Congress

Did Mother Jones and her industrial army march in vain?

Not necessarily. Six years later, in 1909, Pennsylvania passed stronger child labor laws and implemented better means of enforcement. The minimum working age was raised to fourteen, and the maximum number of work hours per week was set at fifty-eight.

Pennsylvania had passed an improved child labor law, but it was still many more years before the federal government enacted effective child labor legislation.

CHAPTER SIX

"BUILD UP YOUR UNION"

Agnes Nestor and the Garment Workers' Strike Chicago (1897), New York City, and Philadelphia (1909–1910)

I n the spring of 1897, when Agnes Nestor was sixteen, her father was out of work. Hoping to find a job as a machinist, he moved his family from Grand Rapids, Michigan, to Chicago, Illinois.

The principal of her school in Grand Rapids hoped that Agnes would finish the eighth grade. She wrote a letter for Agnes to carry to

On the picket line, girls banded together no matter what language they spoke.
Library of Congress

her new school. In the letter, the principal described Agnes as a "good, attentive, and faithful student."

But Agnes never returned to school. Once in Chicago, her older sister, Mary, found a job at a candy factory, while Agnes applied for work at the Eisendrath Glove Company. She had trouble convincing the factory superintendent that she was old enough to work. "I was

Chicago offered work opportunities for Agnes and her older sister, Mary. Library of Congress

small for my age and wore my hair down my back in two small braids," Agnes later wrote in her autobiography. She left the factory convinced that she would never find a job.

A few days later a postcard arrived in the morning mail. It told her to report to the knitting department at the Eisendrath Glove factory and to bring her own apron and scissors.

"I was put to work on a winding machine, winding the yarn onto cones," said Agnes. "If a thread broke, that stopped the whole operation, and I would get a reproving look from the boy who worked with me."

That evening, Agnes told her mother how just one broken thread had stopped the entire winding operation. Her mother, who had worked as a child in a cotton mill, showed Agnes how to make a small weaver's knot that would fit into the machine.

Mrs. Nestor told Agnes how she used to work fourteen-hour days, from

Agnes Nestor gave the appearance of frailty, but she was a tireless organizer. A lawyer said she had a mind like a trip hammer. Chicago Historical Society

five in the morning until nightfall. Once, she told Agnes, she and the other children joined the grown-up workers in a strike. The children tried to explain their grievances to the factory superintendent, but he refused to listen.

"Children were not supposed to have any grievances," Mrs. Nestor told Agnes. "They were not supposed to demand shorter hours for backbreaking work."

Agnes soon learned that employers still didn't listen to young employees, but for a short while, she was contented with her work. The weekly pay for beginners like Agnes was three dollars.

"A Day Has Twelve Coats"

Agnes Nestor's family was suffering. Throughout the nation, other families suffered, too. Many fathers were unemployed; even when fathers had work, they couldn't earn enough to support themselves, let alone an entire family.

But plenty of work existed for women and children, who were paid far less than men. Many worked in the booming garment industry.

During the years 1880 to 1920, the garment industry experienced tremendous growth. Mass production of the sewing machine changed the way clothing was made. Once, sewing had been a craft, and clothing was stitched at home or created in specialized shops. With the use of sewing machines, garment

In the sewing room, factory workers sat at long rows of tables. ILGWU Archives, Kheel Center, Cornell University

factories could produce dresses, shirts, coats, pants, gloves, and other articles of clothing in great numbers.

In the factories, hundreds of girls and women sat at long tables, sewing pieces of clothing for ten or more hours each day. "When I was younger," said one woman, "girls were taught full trades. They made pants, coats, overcoats, and then they learned to cut. Now one stitches the seam, another makes the button holes, and another puts the buttons on."

The piecework system made the workers feel like machines. The fastest pieceworkers set the pace for the rest of the girls in the room; each worker was paid by the number of pieces she finished. While the piecework system

increased the overall production, creating more profit for the employer, it resulted in more demanding work and lower wages for many workers.

Most of the factories were located in the poorest sections of cities like Chicago, New York, and Philadelphia. The old wooden buildings had rickety stairs and splintered and sagging floors. The few windows were seldom washed, and cardboard often replaced broken windowpanes. The lack of ventilation created foul and diseased air. There was usually only one stove to heat the entire room, leaving the girls either too hot or too cold, depending on where they sat. Inflammable material scraps lay about on the floors. Many buildings were firetraps—disasters waiting to happen.

In the factories, the bathrooms were often so filthy that workers refused to use them, which resulted in kidney problems. At one Philadelphia factory, the girls had to pay five cents a week to use the mirror and towel and five cents for water from the faucet. Rats and other vermin were common.

In some garment factories, the girls and women paid fifty cents a week for the use of the sewing machines and electricity. They also had to buy their own needles and machine oil, often at exorbitant prices. In other factories, the girls had to buy their own machines, which they carried strapped to their backs to and from work each day. When one New York City factory burned, all the girls lost their sewing machines. Because the machines weren't covered by insurance, the girls had to pay for the replacements.

Men worked in the garment industry, too, but they usually held the higher-paying positions of cutters. Only men could become cutters or bosses.

Foremen in the garment industry had a reputation for driving their workers.

Some garments were started in the factory, then hired out to "finishers" to be completed for low wages. Photography Collection, University of Maryland Baltimore County

Workers who took too long in the bathroom were fined; workers who arrived five minutes late were docked as much as half a day's pay. Some bosses fined the workers for talking or singing.

Bosses often harassed the female workers, who complained they were groped, grabbed, and pinched. Some girls were afraid to complain, for fear they would be fired.

At some factories, bosses stole time from the workers. "They made us work long hours by moving the hands of the clock when we did not see it," said one girl. "Sometimes we found that we got only twenty minutes [instead of thirty] for lunch and that when the clock showed five, it was really after six."

In order to meet production needs, workers often took garments home to finish. Some workers never went home. They worked at night, sleeping for a few hours on bundles in the shop.

Some factories and small shops determined quitting time by the number of items that were produced. Abraham Cahan managed to find humor in his working conditions: "I get twelve dollars a week, and a working week has six days . . . but a day is neither a Sunday or Monday nor anything unless we make twelve coats. The calendars are a lot of liars. . . . They say a day has twenty-four hours. That's a bluff. A day has twelve coats."

Despite so many hardships, the workers grew deeply loyal to one another. They were all members of a "working class." They wanted to improve their daily lives and the lives of their families. But to accomplish this goal, they needed a union.

"Come on Out!"

At the Eisendrath Glove Company, young Agnes Nestor proved to be a good worker. Within a month after she started in 1897, she was promoted to mending the knit wrists of the gloves. "It was concentrated, monotonous work," said Agnes, "but there were several other girls sitting with me. We used to vie with each other to see who could do the quickest job." After the knitting room, she worked in the sewing room.

The foreman kept careful track of the amount of work the girls did. The more gloves they made, the more he expected. Though not forbidden, talking was discouraged because the foreman claimed it lowered production.

To maintain production, the girls chipped together to buy an alarm clock and hung it on the wall. Now Agnes and her friends worked and talked, all the while keeping an eye on the clock to make sure they finished the set number of gloves each hour.

Slowly, it dawned on Agnes and the other girls that the piecework system took advantage of workers. It pitted the girls against one another and created favoritism. "There were always the 'pacemakers,'" said Agnes. "Their rate of work had to be the rate of work for all of us, if we were to earn a decent wage."

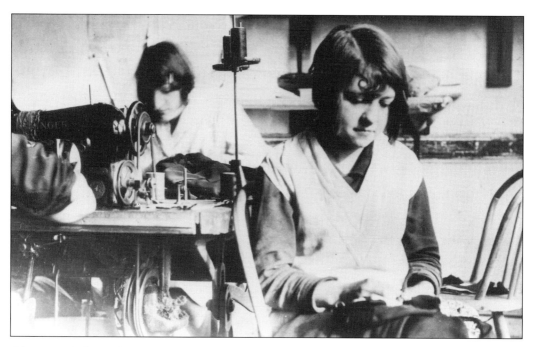

Teenage girls and unmarried women made up seventy percent of the labor force. They handed ninety percent of their salaries over to their parents. ILGWU Archives, Kheel Center, Cornell University

The girls objected to other unjust practices, too. They resented their "machine rent," fifty cents a week for the use of the sewing machines and electricity and the high prices they were charged for the needles and machine oil.

They resented the petty rules. Although the girls wanted to eat lunch with their sisters or friends who worked in other departments, they weren't allowed to leave their assigned rooms. The foreman often spied on the girls to make sure they didn't sneak out of their rooms at lunch.

One day a new system was put in place, requiring each girl to work on even smaller pieces of each glove. The new system was designed to increase the overall production.

But for the girls, piecework was already difficult enough. Smaller pieces increased the tedious nature of the work and also decreased their pay. "We began to think of ways to fight back," said Agnes.

The girls in the banding department walked out in protest against the new system. Although Agnes worked in the sewing room, she and the other sewers feared that the factory would simply hire replacements for the banders. To prevent that from happening, they informed the foremen that they would walk out, too, if the factory tried to hire new banders.

The bosses gave in and abandoned the new system, and the girls returned to work. But the girls also realized that they needed to organize the workers into a union. A union would provide strength and protection for the workers.

After work, Agnes and several others attended their first union meeting. Within a few days after the banders' walkout, most of the shop had signed up for union membership.

Several days later, the girls had an opportunity to test the solidarity of their newly formed union when a fellow worker was unfairly discharged. Outraged, Agnes and the other union sewers formulated a strike plan. "We decided it would be cowardly to walk out at noon," said Agnes. "We would wait until the whistle blew to resume work, and then, as the power started up on the machines, we would begin our exodus."

When the whistle blew, the girls lined up for their walkout. Suddenly, the foreman and several other men entered the room. They had discovered the strike plan. The foreman ordered the girls to return to their work.

Undaunted, Agnes and the girls began to chant: "We are not going to pay rent for our machines!" They filed out of the factory and lined up on the street. They called out the names of the girls who were still working. "Come on out!" they shouted, hoping the other girls would join them.

A few girls emerged from the factory, and then another and another until the entire shop was nearly emptied. The striking girls paraded down the street for a meeting with their union leaders.

At the meeting, the girls listed their demands. No more machine rent. No more paying for needles and machine oil. They wanted raises for the girls who were paid the least. And, most importantly, they wanted their employers to recognize their union.

Union recognition meant that employers and employees would meet, discuss, and reach an understanding of each other's rights and interests. A union would protect the striking girls. Otherwise, once the girls returned to work, the employers could fire anyone they wanted. They knew the strike leaders would be the first to be discharged. Without a union, unfair work conditions would be reinstated.

Despite her young age, Agnes was selected by the union officers to represent the striking girls. When her sister Mary heard that Agnes was elected leader, she was surprised. "Why did they put Agnes on?" said Mary. "She can't talk!" Little did Mary, or even Agnes, know: Agnes's career in union politics began that day.

Agnes and the other strikers picketed daily. They wore buttons on their coats that said, "Organize! I'm with You!" They also held meetings in the town hall, which they had rented.

When the strike entered its second week, the Eisendrath Glove Company offered the strikers a compromise. They promised to restore the girls' old jobs and to eliminate the machine rent and to provide free machine oil. Needles would be sold at cost. The girls in the lowest paid department were offered a one-dollar-a-week raise. But the company didn't offer to recognize the union.

As far as the girls were concerned, the offer was unacceptable without union recognition. They doubled their picket line.

Although most of the girls had joined the strike, one department was missing: the girls from the kid glove department. Kid gloves, made of the finest leather, were the most expensive gloves that the company made. "Like the gloves they made," said Agnes, "the kid glove makers felt they were superior to the rest of us and used to refer haughtily to us as the 'horsehide girls.'"

When one of the kid glove girls tried to cross the picket line to work, the strikers formed a circle around her and refused to let her pass. If she wasn't going to strike, they wanted her to go home. Then a striking girl threatened to duck the kid glove girl in a nearby water trough for horses. Nobody realized that a newspaper reporter was watching.

Bosses watched the girls carefully, even during lunchtime. Culver Pictures

The next day, a front-page story appeared in a Chicago newspaper: "Strikers Duck Girl in Water Trough." Other newspapers picked up the story, and each time it was repeated, it became even more exaggerated, even though the girl had never been ducked. At one point, someone said that a policeman had been ducked by Agnes Nestor!

Even though the newspaper articles were not true, Agnes didn't mind. The newspaper publicity actually helped the girls' cause. Just ten days after the strike had begun, the Eisendrath Glove Factory agreed to the girls' demands, including recognition as a union shop. A union shop meant that new employees were expected to join the union or that the employers would only recruit new workers through the union.

"We went back to work the following Monday with flying colors," said Agnes. "Our union shop was our most important gain."

Entire families sewed at home. To finish one pair of pants, for example, canvas was sewn by hand around the bottom, linings were inserted into the waistband, pockets were tacked, two stays and eight buttons were fastened, six buttonholes were sewn, buckles were attached to a back strap, and finally tickets were attached. All this for seven cents a pair! Photograph Collection, University of Maryland Baltimore County

"If I Turn Traitor"

By 1902, Agnes Nestor had developed a reputation as a keen negotiator for the glovemakers' union, and she had become an impressive speaker.

In 1904, the Women's Trade Union League, which had headquarters in Chicago, invited Agnes to speak at a meeting. The Women's Trade Union League had one main goal: to organize all of the working women in the United States in order to gain better working conditions, reduced hours, a living wage, and full citizenship as women, including the right to vote.

Agnes met Jane Addams, Mary McDowell, Ellen Gates Starr, and others dedicated to improving the working conditions of women. To Agnes, these organizers had great vision and courage. They were unselfishly motivated by a high sense of social justice. Agnes and her friends quickly applied for league membership.

For the next few years, as a member of the Women's Trade Union League, Agnes maintained a hectic speaking schedule. She traveled to other cities and appeared frequently before women's groups, rallying support for improved working conditions and an eight-hour workday.

Agnes visited factories and sweatshops. She discovered that the worst working conditions existed in sweatshops, where unskilled immigrants and their children finished garments that were begun in factories. The more impoverished the worker, the worse the working conditions.

In 1909, the New York City garment industry boasted nearly six hundred shops that employed nearly forty thousand workers. Although some workers were men, most were teenage girls and unmarried women in their early twenties. They worked to help support their immigrant families. Nearly all of them were fed up with the tyrannical bosses, the petty rules, the spying, the favoritism, the low wages, the stiff fines, and the long hours.

Throughout the summer and early fall of 1909, several strikes had erupted. Every day strikers were arrested, fined, and sent to the workhouse, a prison where they served their sentences by scrubbing floors and doing other kinds of labor. In the streets, hired thugs beat the strikers but were never arrested.

Soon it became clear that strikes by individual shops would never succeed. Only an industry-wide strike would create change. Pauline Newman, Rose Schneiderman, and several other young women distributed thousands of circulars written in Yiddish, Italian, and English. The circulars called the garment workers to a mass meeting at Cooper Union in New York City.

On November 22, more than three thousand garment workers crowded into Cooper Union. Labor leaders gave speeches describing the horrors of the garment industry as well as the dangers of rushing into a strike. But to many in the audience, the meeting was all talk. Nothing was getting accomplished.

Suddenly, a young woman called out that she wanted to speak. A tiny,

Fiery Clara Lemlich was barely five feet tall, yet she was a fearless striker.
ILGWU Archives, Kheel Center, Cornell University

fragile woman was lifted onto the platform. She stood, her dark eyes flashing as she spoke in Yiddish: "I have listened to all the speakers. . . . I am one of the ones who feels and suffers from the things pictured. I move that we go on a general strike."

The woman was Clara Lemlich, a twenty-three-year-old garment worker. Strikes were not new to Clara: she had been working and organizing labor unions since she was fifteen. During a strike two months earlier, in September, Clara was arrested seventeen times. Police and company thugs had beat her so severely that they broke six ribs. She hid the bruises from her parents because she didn't want to upset them. "Unions," she admitted later, "aren't built easy."

After Clara spoke, enthusiasm for a general strike swept over the crowd. Men, women, and teenage girls screamed and stamped their feet. They waved their hats and handkerchiefs. They wanted to strike. The outburst lasted nearly five minutes, then silence fell over the hall.

Nearly everyone knew the difficulty that lay ahead. They knew their families depended on their wages. They knew their employers were powerful and influential men. But they cheered one another on. The strike had begun.

The next day, November 23, workers reported to the factories as usual. But they didn't sew. They sat in front of their machines, waiting expectantly. Then, in shop after shop throughout New York City, a union member gave a signal, then pushed off the power button. The lights went out, the machines turned off, and the workers stampeded from nearly five hundred shops in

Manhattan and Brooklyn. By the end of the day, more than twenty thousand girls and women were on strike.

The dramatic strike astonished the nation. Who could think that girls had the strength and courage to walk picket lines? Face arrest? Suffer beatings from police and hired thugs? Pay fines? Endure jail? Yet this is what the teenage girls and young women did, day after day, during the bitter winter months of 1909–1910.

The garment industries fought back by forming the Association of Waist and Dress Manufacturers of New York. They recruited strikebreakers. They hired prostitutes to stand outside the factories and pick fights with the strikers. They sent work to plants in Philadelphia. Company thugs attacked the striking girls with iron bars and sticks. Police used billy clubs. Owners threatened to close their shops and open factories in other states.

In New York City, the Women's Trade Union League was appalled at the way the strikers were treated. They called a mass meeting of all the young women who had been attacked by the police. Teenage girls took their turn on stage to tell how the police beat them or failed to protect them from attack by their bosses. A ten-year-old girl moved the audience to tears.

Despite cruel treatment, the girls remained committed to the cause. By December 20, the strike spread to Philadelphia, where the same deplorable work conditions existed. The Women's Trade Union League needed someone persuasive enough to organize the strikers in Philadelphia.

The League called on Agnes Nestor to help.

"A Soldier"

"I felt like a soldier being called to duty," said Agnes, when she got the call in Chicago. "It was hard to leave home with Christmas only five days away, but there was only one thing for me to say. I agreed to go."

Agnes arrived in Philadelphia, prepared to handle the organizational duties of the strike.

Each day Agnes showed up at the magistrate court to pay the fines or the

Between November 23 and December 25, 1909, more than 700 striking women and girls were arrested. ILGWU Archives, Kheel Center, Cornell University

bail of arrested picketers. Most girls were fined five dollars, but some magistrates fined the girls ten dollars or gave them ten days in jail. When necessary, Agnes hired attorneys and followed the cases to court. She found women to replace the arrested girls on the picket lines.

In Philadelphia, as well as in New York City, the strikers were helped by groups of well-to-do women who were dedicated to social reform. The "Mink Brigade," as these women were called, set up food kitchens and relief stations. They contributed funds and paid the arrested strikers' bail and fines. They also marched on the picket line. For the first time, many Mink Brigade members learned what life was like for working-class women.

Some members of the Mink Brigade were college students. Others were women such as Helen Taft, daughter of the president of the United States; the heiress Anne Morgan; Mrs. Gifford Pinchot, wife of the future governor of

Pennsylvania; and Frances Cochran, daughter of a wealthy Philadelphia family. In the eyes of the upper class, their support lent respectability to the strike.

One day, a police officer arrested Frances Cochran and another striker who were marching in a picket line. Frances's arrest caused quite a stir, and the embarrassed officer wanted to release her at once. But Frances refused, unless he released the other girl, too. "We were both doing the same thing," said Frances. "We were walking up and down the street. Therefore, we should both be treated alike." Both young women were released.

When other policemen realized that they were arresting socially prominent women, they were worried. One of the officers said, "Why didn't you tell me you was a rich lady? I'd never have arrested you in the world." Many people wondered why working girls could be clubbed but not women who wore mink.

Wealthy members of the Women's Trade Union League, called the Mink Brigade, joined the strikers on the picket line. Library of Congress

During a mass meeting at Carnegie Hall, New York City, strikers gathered to protest police brutality. The strikers wore banners that said "Arrested." ILGWU Archives, Kheel Center, Cornell University

The Philadelphia strike hit the big New York manufacturers hard. They had counted on the Philadelphia garment workers to fill their orders. Now who would sew their shirt-waists?

The New York Manufacturers' Association decided to seek a settlement with the New York strikers. They offered them their jobs back, along with a fifty-two-hour workweek, higher wages, prompt consideration of grievances, four paid holidays, and no charges for needles, thread, and appliances. But they refused to recognize the union.

The striking girls and women refused the offer. They knew the importance of union recognition. "[The bosses] can't fool us," said a seventeen-year-old Russian girl. "We know without the union, they will treat us like before."

"Of course the bosses don't understand the sympathy we have for each other," said another young girl, who also emigrated from Russia. "One girl for all girls. The union is what will make us strong and nothing else."

Still another sixteen-year-old Russian girl

said: "I think the union is like a mother and father to the children. I'd give my whole life for the union. Why shouldn't we have as much rights as men?"

The strike wore on into January. More strikers continued to be arrested. More fines and more bail had to be paid. Agnes Nestor and other League members grew worried as funds became scarce. Some days it seemed as though no settlement would ever be reached.

The strikers were becoming worn out, too. Many had pawned their bracelets, earrings, pins, and whatever valuables they owned. Some were eating only one meal a day, if that.

By the end of January, many of the larger New York City shops had settled, one by one, with the worn-out strikers. The New York Triangle Shirtwaist factory workers still held out. So did the Philadelphia workers. The strike dragged on into February.

On February 5, Agnes Nestor and the other organizers were sitting around the fireplace. The strike seemed hopeless. Agnes was due back in Chicago, but she didn't want to desert the strikers. As the organizers sat, wondering aloud what to do, Agnes reminded the others, "It is always darkest before the dawn."

The next morning, the Philadelphia employers offered a settlement: a fifty-two-and-a-half-hour week, increased wages, a board of arbitration, and no fees for power, machine straps, or needles.

By February 15, the strike was officially called off. "The strikers hailed the settlement as a great victory," said Agnes. "When Mrs. Robins and I came onto the platform, and after each of us had spoken, there was wild cheering and clapping for a full five minutes. We considered it a meeting long to be remembered."

Build Up Your Union
But Agnes Nestor and other members of the Women's Trade Union League knew the victory wasn't complete. The strikers had hoped for a greater wage increase and union recognition in all shops, but they were forced back

to work because they had run out of money. Some girls returned to work with few or no gains. But Agnes Nestor knew that in most shops the settlement was the best the strikers could do at the time. She told the girls to build up their union so that next time they would be in a position to get better terms.

The Philadelphia and New York City contracts had also failed to address or negotiate many important safety concerns. At the Triangle Shirtwaist Company, for instance, the strikers had asked for better safety precautions. The factory occupied the upper three floors of a ten-story building. The factory rooms were poorly ventilated. Pieces of fabric and oil-soaked rags littered the floors.

During work hours, the bosses bolted all but one door from the outside. Employees had to enter and exit through the same door so the bosses could search the girls at the end of the day to ensure they weren't stealing ribbon or lace. The locked doors also prevented workers from taking unexcused bathroom breaks. A freight elevator provided the only other exit.

When a fire broke out at the factory on March 25, 1911, barely a year after the shirtwaist strike was settled, workers were locked inside the burning building. Some of the trapped workers jumped from the windows. "I looked up," said William Shepherd, a reporter, "and saw that there were scores of girls at the windows. The flames from the floor below were beating in their faces."

Shepherd continued, "I watched one girl falling, waving her arms, trying to keep her body upright. Until the very instant she struck the sidewalk, she was trying to balance herself. Then came the thud—then a silent, unmoving pile of clothing and twisted broken limbs."

At one window, Shepherd noticed a young man standing on the ledge. He helped girl after girl to the windowsill, then held her away from the building and let her drop. "Undoubtedly the young man saw that a terrible death awaited them in the flames," said the reporter. "His was only a terrible chivalry.

The Triangle Shirtwaist Company occupied the top three floors of this ten-story building. When a fire broke out, many workers jumped to their death rather than be burned alive. ILGWU Archives, Kheel Center, Cornell University

Two victims of the fire, probably sisters, are shown in this photograph taken before their death. ILGWU Archives, Kheel Center, Cornell University

Dozens of girls died when they hit the pavement. Others were burned alive, while still others died from smoke inhalation. In all, 146 workers, mostly women and girls, died.

William Shepherd remembered their great strike the year before. "The same girls had demanded more sanitary conditions and safety precautions in the shops," he said. "Their dead bodies were the answer."

CHAPTER SEVEN

"THEY UNDERSTOOD THE STOMACH LANGUAGE"

The Lawrence Strike (1912)

Pretty, dark-haired Camella Teoli was the twelve-year-old daughter of Italian immigrants. One day in 1909, a man visited her house in Lawrence, Massachusetts. He asked her father why Camella went to school instead of to work at one of the Lawrence mills.

Although Camella's father knew her age, he told the man: "I don't know whether she is thirteen or fourteen years old."

"You give me four dollars," said the man, "and I will make the paper come from the old country saying she is fourteen."

It was said that a mile of mills stretched along the Merrimack River in Lawrence, Massachusetts. Immigrant City Archives, Lawrence, Massachusetts

Four dollars was a lot of money to the large Teoli family, but her father was eager for Camella to work. He paid the man, and in one month the papers arrived. As promised, they certified that Camella was fourteen.

Camella began to work in the spinning department at a Lawrence mill. She changed spools on a machine that twisted cotton yarn. She had to learn quickly. Those who couldn't keep up were fired.

New workers like Camella didn't get paid as they learned the job.

The bosses said they hindered the experienced workers and slowed down the production.

Within two weeks, Camella knew the job, and the machine was speeded up. Just before quitting time one day, a terrible accident occurred. While the machines were still running, Camella unpinned her long hair. It spilled over her shoulders and down her back. She bent over and began to comb the hair over her head. A fellow worker, a boy, called to her. She stood and tossed her hair back.

The spinning machine grabbed Camella's hair and sucked it into the gears. The machine was too fast and too powerful for Camella, who was unable to stop it or disentangle herself. The gears gobbled up the hair and tore off two large sections of her scalp.

Hearing her screams, another worker raced over and shut off the machine. Workers picked Camella up and rushed her to the hospital. Someone picked up the two large pieces of scalp, wrapped them in newspaper, and took them to the hospital, too. Camella spent the next seven months in the hospital. Her father was arrested for falsifying her age.

Nearly three years later, during the Lawrence strike of 1912, Camella's story became front-page news throughout the country when she and fifteen other children were called to testify before the United States Senate. President William Howard Taft asked to meet the Lawrence children. He wanted to hear their stories. So did senators, congressmen, and the American public.

In Washington, Camella sat in front of the House committee. She wore her hair in a bun to hide the permanent bald spot at the back of her head. She told the House committee how her father got the papers that falsified her age, how the machine grabbed her hair, and how the company paid the hospital bills but none of the wages she lost.

Mrs. William Howard Taft, wife of the president, sat in the audience. Newspapers all over the country reported how the First Lady stayed all morning, listening "with great interest" to Camella and the other children. She heard them describe their living and working conditions and accounts of the strike.

One-half of the Lawrence children between the ages of fourteen and eighteen worked in the textile mills. It took the wages of an entire family to survive.

Immigrant City Archives, Lawrence, Massachusetts

She heard the adult strikers tell how pregnant women were clubbed and beaten by the militia during the strike. Horrified, she rushed from the room.

The children's testimonies helped the Lawrence workers win their strike. The newspaper headlines embarrassed the mill owners and Lawrence city officials, who didn't want people to know how they treated their employees. The Lawrence strike was considered the most militant and most organized in labor history.

"Better to Starve Fighting"

Terrible working and living conditions existed in Lawrence. Many families were slowly starving, even though they worked fifty-four hours a week. Daily meals, for the most part, consisted of bread, molasses, and beans. Most mill families couldn't afford milk, and nearly all the children wanted to stay in school, but their families needed their wages.

"I would have kept on with school," fifteen-year-old Charles Vasiersky told the House Committee, "but we did not have anything to eat, and so I had to go to work."

Fourteen-year-old John Boldelar said: "What would we eat if I went to school? Some horses live better than we do."

The mill families lived in squalid tenements where rats carried off anything edible. Medical authorities estimated that disease and poverty killed nearly one out of every five children of Lawrence mill families before their first birthday, not counting the many babies that died at birth.

The working conditions were especially difficult for women and young girls. Mothers, desperate for money, worked right up until a few hours before their babies were born. Some mothers gave birth between the rows of looms. Women and young girls also suffered sexual harassment and verbal abuse from their bosses.

All workers resented the "premium" or "bonus" system as well as the unbearable speedups. Under the bonus system, workers had to produce a standard amount of work each day for four weeks. If a worker failed to meet

The immigrant mill workers lived in narrow, wooden tenements. Some tenements were so close together that landlords simply leaned across the air shafts to collect the rent. Immigrant City Archives, Lawrence, Massachusetts

the standard or lost a day's work for illness, the bonus was lost—even if the worker had surpassed the standard on all other days during the period. The bonus was eight percent of the worker's pay.

Many immigrants thought conditions couldn't get worse, but they did. In 1912, a new Massachusetts law created a fifty-four-hour workweek for women and children instead of fifty-six. The law was intended to help, but it actually hurt the Lawrence workers.

Women and children comprised more than half of the Lawrence working force. Since the hour limit affected so many employees, the mill operators decided to shorten the men's workweek, too. At the same time, the mill operators speeded up the machines so the workers would produce the same amount of cloth.

"They were trying to make up the two hours," said Samuel Lipson, a twenty-nine year old Russian immigrant. "And they tried to speed up the machinery in order to make us do fifty-six hours' work in fifty-four hours' time."

Because the workers' production was the same, they hoped that their wages would stay the same. But the wages were lowered. "They cut down the wages after they speeded up the machinery," said Lipson. "We thought we would have to starve."

Samuel Lipson said that the wage cut sent a message from the workers' stomachs to their heads: "The stomach telephoned the head. 'I cannot stand molasses any longer for butter and bananas for meat.'"

Lawrence was an immigrant city, where nearly fifty different languages and dialects were spoken. Most immigrants did not understand English. "But they understood the stomach language," said Samuel Lipson.

The new Massachusetts law became effective on January 1, 1912. For two weeks, the workers remained hopeful as they waited for their first pay envelope. They knew that the mills were still making great profits. They hoped the operators would not cut their wages.

On January 11, a group of Polish women at the Everett Mill were the first to get their wages. When they opened their pay envelopes, they saw that their wages had been cut. "Not enough pay! Not enough pay!" they cried. The pay reduction was equal to the cost of four loaves of bread—bread that their children desperately needed.

The women's cry spread throughout Everett Mill. As more workers realized that their wages were cut, the anger grew. "[The workers] were desperate," said Samuel Lipson, "seeing the children barefooted, seeing their women not having clothes to go out in such cold weather, and still [the mill owners] were trying to take away the piece of bread from their mouths."

Rage had been building among the workers for a long time. They hated the mill system, the poor wages, the poor living conditions, the out-of-work fathers, the broken family spirit, and the loss of old-world pride. The pay cut was the last insult.

"Better to starve fighting than to starve working," the Italian men cried. They ran from room to room, shutting off the power. They grabbed knives and slashed the machine belts and shredded the finished cloth. They smashed windows and lightbulbs and even pulled workers from their machines. They hurled bobbins and shuttles at anyone who dared to work.

The riot alarm sounded from the bell tower of the Lawrence city hall. The police were called out, but still the strike spread. By nightfall, ten thousand children, women, and men were on strike. Two days later, the strikers numbered more than twenty-three thousand. By Monday, January 15, Lawrence was an armed camp. The machines were silent.

Samuel Lipson was right. Every immigrant worker understood the stomach language. The stomach language had fused them together. Now they were united to fight a common enemy: poverty.

"The Only Way We Can Teach Them"

For the first two days, striking workers roamed through the city streets. They had succeeded in stopping the machinery of the largest textile center in the world. They had galvanized the largest-ever strike force. But now what? The mill owners had city officials, the police, and even the state militia on their side.

The first confrontation occurred on Monday, January 15, a cold wintry day. The mill owners tried to keep the workers from picketing. As strikers crossed a bridge to reach a mill on the other side, police and militia waited with fire hoses. The police and militia blasted the strikers with cold water.

Most of the soaking wet strikers retreated, but some stayed, determined to fight. They picked up chunks of ice and whipped them at the soldiers. Others pelted the soldiers with snowballs. A group of women caught a soldier crossing the bridge. They tore off his uniform and tried to throw the nearly naked man into the icy canal. He managed to wrench himself free and escape.

But the strikers were outnumbered. The police quickly arrested thirty-six people, who were immediately sent to jail for one year. "The only way we can teach them is to deal out the severest sentences," said the judge.

Some newspapers called the confrontation a "Bayonet Charge on Lawrence Strikers," although it was more of a snowball fight. The skirmish was just what city officials wanted. They declared that the strike had

The first confrontation occurred when the soldiers hosed the strikers with cold water as they attempted to cross the canal bridge. The Archives of Labor and Urban Affairs, Wayne State University

reached "crisis" proportions. They ordered the troops to use whatever force was necessary to quell disturbances, even shoot to kill.

Samuel Lipson and many other immigrants were educated in their homeland. In the old country, they had learned the importance of soup kitchens,

relief funds, publicity, and mass meetings. But to accomplish these things in Lawrence, they needed organization and strong leadership. Who would help?

Not the United Textile Workers. They called the strike "revolutionary" and "anarchistic." Not the American Federation of Labor either.

At first, the Women's Trade Union League had opened relief stations to give food and clothing to more than eight thousand strikers. But the League worked only in agreement with the United Textile Workers. When the United Textile Workers refused to become involved, the women withdrew their aid.

The Industrial Workers of the World (I.W.W. or Wobblies) stepped in. They sent their best organizers to Lawrence: Joseph Ettor, Arturo Giovannetti, Bill Haywood, and Elizabeth Gurley Flynn.

The I.W.W. envisioned a utopian, classless society. They believed in one big industrial union of all workers, men and women, black and white. Many considered the I.W.W. a militant group, known for answering "fire with fire, gunshot with gunshot . . . and marching off to jail defiantly." But Joseph Ettor implored the Lawrence strikers, "Make this strike as peaceful as possible." He reminded them that the militia and mill owners "cannot weave cloth with bayonets. . . . In the last analysis, all the blood spilled will be your blood."

With the help of the I.W.W. leaders, the strikers organized. They presented four clear demands to the mill owners: a fifteen-percent wage increase, time-and-a-half overtime pay, an end to the premium or bonus system, and no discrimination in rehiring strikers after the dispute ended.

The picket line became an effective nonviolent strike strategy. Workers walked picket lines continuously outside the mills, twenty-four hours a day. At times, as many as twenty thousand men, women, and children picketed. They formed a human chain, which no scab worker could penetrate. When the pickets were ordered to leave, they lay down or sat in peaceful demonstration.

Sometimes the strikers paraded through the city. They linked arms and tramped down the width of the sidewalks, sweeping aside anyone they met. They passed in and out of stores, which terrorized the shopkeepers and kept customers home.

They also sang. No matter where the strikers were—at strike meetings, soup kitchens, or on the street—they sang. The singing boosted their morale and bonded the nationalities together in a religious fervor.

Despite the nonviolent strike measures, Ettor's prediction came true. The strikers' blood was spilled during another major confrontation on January 29.

In an attempt to trick the strikers into returning to work, the mill owners spread rumors that the strike was over. They even started up the machines so people could hear them running. When strikers heard the rumors, they marched through the streets to show that they were not working. The police ordered them to disperse, but the strikers found themselves boxed in—police on one side and militia on the other.

Tempers flared. People shouted, shoved, and pushed, not knowing which way to go. Then a shot rang out. It struck Annie LoPizzo in the heart. She died instantly.

Although Annie was a striker, she wasn't parading that day. She was on her way to visit a friend when she got caught between the strikers and the police. Nineteen witnesses claimed that they saw the militiaman who fired the gun, but he was never arrested. Instead, the police arrested strike leaders Ettor and Giovannetti, who were three miles away at the time, and charged them as accessories to the murder. Joseph Caruso, a parading striker, was also arrested, charged with inciting and provoking violence.

After the Annie LoPizzo murder, the strikers rioted. They pulled trolley cars off tracks. They smashed trolley windows and dragged passengers from

After the death of Annie LoPizzo, strikers rioted. Immigrant City Archives, Lawrence, Massachusetts

their seats. "Any man, woman, or child giving any appearance of going to work was attacked, knocked down, kicked, and clubbed," said a reporter for the *New York Times.* "Dinner pails were snatched from hands, spilled out, and the contents trampled. The strikers tore coats and overalls off the victims."

The strikers visited the homes of scab workers. They painted black hands on the scabs' houses and painted the word "scab" in bright red letters. They threw stones through windows and left letters that threatened the safety of any worker who dared to cross the picket line. The home of a police officer was set on fire.

Throughout the strike, more casualties occurred. A Syrian boy, John Rami, died after he was stabbed in the back with a bayonet. It pierced his lung. Several other strikers were also stabbed with bayonets, but they survived.

Soldiers were ordered to use whatever force was necessary to quell any disturbance.
The Archives of Labor and Urban Affairs, Wayne State University

Mothers and their children were clubbed. Two pregnant women were beaten so badly that they lost their babies and nearly died.

The district attorney explained why the brutality was necessary: "One policeman can handle ten men," he said, "but it takes ten policemen to handle one woman."

Even dogs weren't safe. "When a striker went along the street with a little dog," said Samuel Lipson, "the soldier stabbed the dog with his bayonet."

Some people incited violence. When armed soldiers held their guns cocked as they faced a crowd of demonstrators, a newspaper reporter yelled, "Fire!" Some reporters made up stories to create news. And someone planted dynamite in three different locations. The strikers were blamed for the dynamite.

"We Are Waiting for That Answer Still"

Many newspapers and editors sided with the mill owners and police. They didn't allow sympathetic coverage of the strike. When one Boston reporter wrote a story that sympathized with the strikers, her editor crumpled it up and threw it at her. The reporter quit and moved to Lawrence to work for the strike committee.

Editorials labeled the strikers "anarchists" who didn't deserve sympathy. "When strikers call for 'smashing the machinery,' they are actually calling for smashing the Constitution and the framework of society on the grounds of social injustice," claimed one editorial writer.

Others called the strike leaders "unscrupulous agitators" who preyed on the ignorance of the immigrants. "The majority of these foreigners are honest, thrifty, well-meaning people," wrote the Lawrence director of public safety. "[T]here would have been no trouble . . . if the agitators had not hastened here and deliberately excited [the immigrants] against the authorities and against the American flag."

Mill owners, other members of the wealthy classes, and even many church clergy claimed that the I.W.W. had stirred up the workers. Officials believed that they could settle the strike on their own. Cardinal Farley agreed, saying, "A fatherly interest and sympathetic relations between employer and employee would solve the entire difficulty."

But the workers didn't want "fathers" who would take care of them as if they were children. They wanted a living wage so that they could take care of themselves and their families. They wanted their children to have the same opportunities as other children. Still, they wondered: where were the "fatherly interest and sympathetic relations" before the strike, when the workers tried to tell their employers how unbearable the working conditions were?

The strike was a last resort. Before it began, the workers at the American Woolen Company had written a letter to the company's president. "We sent a special delivery letter to Mr. Wood, telling him how it was in Lawrence," said Samuel Lipson. "We expected to get an answer because it was a special delivery letter. We are waiting for that answer still."

Mr. Wood explained his position to the *Commercial and Financial Chronicle*: "To pay for fifty-four hours' work the wages of fifty-six would be equivalent to an increase in wages, and that the mills cannot afford to pay." At the time, his company showed a net profit of nearly four million dollars.

"Strikers! Strikers! Strikers!"

Even though many newspapers refused to print sympathetic stories, some did. As news of the strike traveled, workers nationwide sent money to the Lawrence strikers. As much as one thousand dollars poured in each day. Entire towns took up collections and donated money, food, and clothing. Nearby Lowell sent a live cow.

The strike committee used the money to set up eleven soup kitchens, where children and their families could be assured of a hot meal each day. They also established a relief fund: each striking family received from two to five dollars each week. Two doctors donated medical assistance.

Lawrence Children Outside a "Kitchen," Waiting for It to Open

7 O'Clock Dinner 30 Supper 4 30
FREE FOR CHILDREN ONLY

Strikers knew the strategic value of soup kitchens, public relation campaigns, and picket lines. Immigrant City Archives, Lawrence, Massachusetts

Yet parents began to fear for their children's safety and well-being. They decided to send their youngest children away to friendly families in other towns, the way children in the old country were often removed during unpredictable and difficult times. The children would receive good meals and warm homes, and more parents could walk picket lines.

An exodus of children also meant publicity. People all over the country would see the living and working conditions that the mill families, especially the children, endured. In this way, the children would help the strike cause.

Seven hundred people in New York City, Philadelphia, and Barre, Vermont, applied for the children. Committees interviewed prospective families carefully. Although many well-to-do families offered to care for the children, only working-class families were accepted. The strikers wanted to show solidarity among all workers.

On February 10, the first group of children arrived in New York City. At

When the Lawrence children arrived in New York City, thousands turned out to greet them, and a brass band played. Immigrant City Archvies, Lawrence, Massachusetts

Grand Central Station, five thousand people turned out to welcome 119 boys and girls. As the train's searchlight came into view, people hummed "La Marseillaise," the stirring French national anthem composed during the French Revolution. Like the French revolutionaries, the strikers were fighting for ideals of liberty, equality, and brotherhood. They waved red flags with black borders. The black borders were added to the Socialist flags as marks of mourning for Annie LoPizzo and John Rami, the two strikers who had been killed.

As the train approached, the crowd strained against the ropes for a better view. The train pulled into the station, and the doors opened. Two by two, the children emerged and stood on the concrete platform. On signal, they chanted: "Who are we, who are we, who are we! Yes we are, yes we are, yes we are! Strikers! Strikers! Strikers!" The crowd cheered.

As the children descended the platform, the people realized just how pathetic conditions were in Lawrence. The children had no luggage, no suitcases or other parcels, for they were wearing all they owned. Although it was winter, most had no overcoats. They wore thin dresses and shirts and worsted wool caps.

A nurse, Margaret Sanger, noted that the children looked pale and thin and showed signs of malnutrition. "When they had supper it brought tears to my eyes to see them grab the meat with their hands to eat it," she said. Of all the children, only four had underwear. From a town that produced the most and finest cloth in the world, the children of its workers had the least cloth to keep them warm.

On February 17, another group of children left Lawrence. By then, the adverse publicity embarrassed the Lawrence city officials. They called the exodus an "un-American . . . unnecessary war measure, which hurt the community's pride."

The Lawrence authorities also claimed that strike leaders forced parents to send their children away or else lose their relief funds. Others claimed that children were taken against their parents' wishes or that children ran away and sneaked aboard the train, excited at the prospect of seeing the big city.

The strike committee insisted that none of the authorities' concerns or stories were true. All parents had given permission and all had weighed the issue very carefully. The parents believed that the children were safer in other cities where no soldiers patrolled the streets.

"I receive letters from my children," said one mother, "saying that they are happy, that they have new clothes, and they are eating every day as much as they used to eat at home on Sunday."

Letters from children were read publicly at the strike meetings. "We received letters from my child, saying he is enjoying the best days of his life," said Samuel Lipson. "In New York, they sent him to school."

Lawrence officials grew determined to keep the children from leaving. According to Samuel Lipson, policemen visited parents and demanded that they send for their children. The police told one woman, "If you are not going to call the children, we are going to put you out of the house."

On February 23, the Lawrence marshal declared that no more children would be permitted to leave Lawrence, not even with their parents' permission. The next morning, when 150 children and their parents arrived at the station, they were met by 200 militiamen and police, who told them: "You are not going to send any children away this morning."

Most parents became afraid and changed their minds, but forty parents remained convinced that their children would be safer elsewhere. They bought the children's tickets and proceeded

through the station to board the train. The soldiers guarded the station doors, inside and outside, leaving the parents and children no way to escape.

"As soon as the children started out," said Samuel Lipson, "[the soldiers] tried to grab one child from the mother and to grab the women, trying to arrest the children. . . . One policeman took a child and threw her into the wagon and she got a black eye. She was seven years old. Even women being in the family way were arrested and dragged and pushed into the patrol wagon."

Max Bogatin, a salesman, was also horrified. "I saw them take little chil-

As more children left Lawrence, the adverse publicity embarrassed city officials.
Library of Congress

dren and pick them up by the leg and throw them in the patrol wagon like they were mere rags. One of the women put up a little resistance and a policeman grabbed her by the neck and choked her until she was not able to resist anymore."

At the police station, the mothers were charged with neglect and improper guardianship and sent to jail. Sixteen children were taken from their mothers and sent to the poor farm.

When the strikers heard the news, they hurried to the police station. Police held the angry crowd back, preventing them from entering the station.

Newspapers reported the incident. The brutality shocked the country. How could anyone beat innocent children? Prevent parents from doing what they thought was best? Take children from their mothers and send them to the poor farm? Put mothers and their babies in jail?

Americans were outraged. How could this happen in America? They demanded answers. The uproar reached Congress, who called for a federal investigation.

"He Wanted to Know"

As part of the federal investigation, the House committee called for a delegation of strikers to testify before Congress. Early in March, the strike committee selected fifty adult strikers and sixteen child strikers to represent the different ethnic groups.

On the way to Washington, the train carrying the children made several stops. People met the train and brought doughnuts and cake for the children. Donations of money were given to the chaperones. In Washington, the children and their chaperones stayed in a hotel.

Rosario Contarino remembered meeting William Howard Taft, president of the United States. "He was a nice, big man," said Rosario. "He sat at a nice big desk at the White House. He asked us children where we emigrated from, and he wanted to know how the situation was in Lawrence. We told him about the conditions, that people were starving, and that there was no money. We ate in soup kitchens. We got just enough to eat to live." According to Rosario, President Taft gave the chaperones a thousand dollars for the children.

The investigation began. In front of the House committee, Rosario Contarino, Camella Teoli, Charles Vasiersky, and thirteen others showed their pay envelopes to the senators and congressmen. The children described the poverty that had forced them to quit school in order to work. They told how they were still hungry, despite working fifty-four hours a week.

President William Howard Taft asked to see the delegation of strike children.
Library of Congress

If the city officials and mill owners were embarrassed before, the federal investigation made it worse. Once again, stomach language was understood by all who listened to the children's testimony.

The unfavorable publicity forced the American Woolen Company of Lawrence to yield. Over three months after the strike began, the company conceded to the strikers' demands.

On March 18, twenty-five thousand Lawrence men, women, and children gathered on the Lawrence town green to vote their approval of their new contract. They won twenty-five percent wage increases, with the lowest-paid workers getting the largest portion of the increase. They won a fifty-four-hour workweek, with no cut in pay. The bonus system was still in place: over a given period of time, workers still had to produce a set amount of work or else give up their bonus. But the period of time was reduced to two weeks instead of four. The company further agreed that no striker would be discriminated against when rehired after the strike. The American Woolen Company also raised wages in their mills in thirty-three other cities.

By the end of March, other Lawrence mill companies matched the offer. However, strike leaders Ettor, Giovannetti, and Caruso were still in jail. In September, eight months after their arrest, they went to trial and were found not guilty. An agent for the American Woolen Company admitted that the textile mill owners were guilty of hatching the dynamite plot. After his confession, the agent committed suicide.

As for the children who left Lawrence? They returned from New York

When the strike was over and the children returned home, forty thousand people celebrated with a victory parade.
The Archives of Labor and Urban Affairs, Wayne State University

City, Philadelphia, and Vermont on a special train. Forty thousand people greeted them at the station. As the children disembarked from the train, six brass bands played jubilantly. The children's arms were filled with toys, presents, and clothing from their foster families.

The children rode in picnic wagons from the station to Ford's Hall, the former strike headquarters, and the huge crowd paraded behind the wagons. The homecoming was celebrated by all.

CHAPTER EIGHT

"NOW I HAVE A PAST"

The National Child Labor Committee (1904)

The children who worked in an East Side jacket sweatshop in New York City earned between two and three dollars a week. They worked twelve or more hours a day, often seven days a week, pulling the basting threads from the sewn jackets.

"While the [adult] operators are workin' on them jackets, we must keep turnin' the sleeves and the flaps and the collars," said Harry Gladstone. "Sometimes three or four operators commence to holler at us, so we get mixed up and nearly go crazy tryin' to attend to them all. But the boss, he don' care; he pays us the same."

This twelve-year-old boy is pulling basting threads in a New York City sweatshop. Library of Congress

Fifteen-year-old Harry Gladstone had immigrated to America when he was seven. He attended school for three years, where he learned English. At ten, he quit school to work in a sweatshop.

The boys and girls who worked with Harry were dissatisfied with their hours and their wages. "We want a dollar for each machine and no more'n nine hours a day," said Harry. "That's enough, ain't it?"

Harry knew they would never win a strike unless they formed a union. He organized seventy-five "basting pullers" into a children's union, earning the nickname "Boy Organizer." And in August 1898 they went on strike.

Exact terms of the settlement are not known, but the children did win their strike. Despite the win, Harry knew their work wasn't over. To maintain a strong union, they had to continue to stick together and meet regularly.

Before one union meeting, a reporter asked Harry what he planned to tell the girls and boys. At first Harry said he didn't have much to say because he wasn't much of a speaker. But after he thought a moment, he told the reporter: "I'll tell them to stick together and to think about their poor fathers and mothers they have got to support. I'll speak to them of the schools and how they can't go there to get their education, but must spend . . . [their] day in a pest-hole, pulling bastings, turning collars and sleeves, and running around as if they are crazy."

Later, Harry spoke to his fellow workers, children as young as he had been when he started to work in a sweatshop. Like him, they had quit school and worked to help support their families. He grew emotional as he told them: "If you don't look out for yourselves, who will? You have not had time to grow up, to get strength for work, when you must spend your dearest days in a sweatshop. . . The only way to get the bosses to pay us good wages is to stick together, so let us be true to our union."

Harry knew that change was impossible without a union.

Not All Kids

Not all kids could form unions and go on strike. Before the Civil War, slave children performed many of the same jobs that free children did, but under greatly different conditions. They made significant contributions to the growth and development of the United States.

Most slaves worked on farms and plantations, but some—about five

The northern cotton mills' demand for cotton resulted in an increased amount of cotton production and the expansion of slavery. By 1860, nearly five billion bales of cotton were produced each year. Library of Congress

percent—worked in mines or in cotton, tobacco, sugar, and hemp factories. Many slaves who worked in southern factories were children. No matter where they worked, slave children could not organize unions and negotiate with their employers, the way free children could.

Some people thought that the white children who worked in factories, mines, and mills were treated like slaves, but when white children worked, they received wages, however meager. They could divide their time between school and work. White children often worked alongside their parents, without fear of being traded or sold. If they didn't like their employers or working or living conditions, they could quit. And it was easier for white children to run away.

Many slaves found ways to protest and resist, despite harsh punishments. Some escaped. Some resisted quietly, in small daily acts of living and sabotage. Others protested violently, risking their lives to rebel against the worst

Five percent of all slaves worked in southern factories like this tobacco factory. Many factory slaves were children. Library of Congress

kind of human oppression. The rebels showed extraordinary courage and determination.

During the Reconstruction period after the Civil War, cotton mills were built throughout the South. Mill owners hoped that industrialization would create great wealth and help rebuild the South. The factory and mill work was intended to benefit impoverished whites, and blacks were not hired. Early unions excluded black children and their parents from membership. Many years passed before equitable work and union opportunities became available to African Americans.

The National Child Labor Committee
As the number of industries continued to grow, so did the number of working children. By 1900, a United States census revealed that nearly two million

African American children usually weren't employed in the cotton mills but worked as sharecroppers or tenant farmers. Library of Congress

girls and boys between the ages of ten and sixteen worked. The number was probably greater because the census didn't count children under age ten who worked illegally.

An Alabama minister, the Reverend Edgar Gardner Murphy, became concerned about the number of poor white children working in the southern mills. He initiated the formation of the National Child Labor Committee in 1904. A believer in states' rights, Murphy wanted the states to pass uniform child labor legislation, but he didn't want federal laws. He resigned when it became apparent that committee members were lobbying for federal child labor laws.

Yet the National Child Labor Committee was born with one main goal:

Lewis Hine photographed these two tiny workers in a southern hosiery mill.
Library of Congress

to abolish child labor in the United States. To accomplish this, committee members gathered as much evidence as they could about the extent and nature of child labor. They investigated the industries and trades notorious for hiring large numbers of children: glass factories, textile mills, coal mines, canneries, as well as the street trades and field work. They published articles and stories about working children in newspapers and magazines.

In 1906, the National Child Labor Committee (NCLC) realized that stories weren't enough. They also needed photographs. They hired the photographer Lewis Hine to document the plight of working children. The idea was unique: most photographers didn't photograph the working class because it wasn't profitable. Only the middle and upper classes could afford to buy photographs. Who would want pictures of poor workers?

But the NCLC believed in the importance of the photographs. They knew

Hine noted that the carry-in boy in a Virginia glass factory worked the day shift one week and the night shift the next. Another reformer noted that the glass factory owners often built fences around their properties to "keep the boys in at night."
Library of Congress

that the pictures would arouse public opinion against child labor. Lewis Hine agreed.

At first Hine worked as a freelance photographer, getting paid for each photograph he produced. The photographs were published in newspapers, magazines, and pamphlets that the NCLC distributed. The more working children he saw, the more he believed that child labor had to be eradicated. By 1908, he was working full-time for the NCLC, traveling throughout the United States.

Hine photographed the boys who worked in the glass factories, where the high temperatures and noxious fumes ruined their eyes and caused lung diseases. He photographed the breaker boys bent over coal chutes and other

This seven-year-old girl began shucking oysters at the age of five. Photography Collection, University of Maryland Baltimore County

young mine workers who lost arms and legs due to accidents. In textile mills, he photographed barefoot boys and girls, some with missing fingers. He photographed the tiny cannery children who stood on boxes to reach the table. He photographed messengers, delivery boys, and newsies working at all hours of the day and night. He photographed the workers in sweatshops, in tenement houses, and in sugar beet fields, cotton fields, and cranberry bogs.

It wasn't easy. Bosses and supervisors often refused Hine access to their worksites. Parents and employers lied about the true ages of the children. Even the children lied.

But Hine was determined. He sneaked into mills and factories during the early hours before the bosses arrived. At other times, he posed as a fire inspector or a salesman. Once inside, he pretended to photograph the building or the machinery, not the children. He often guessed at a child's age by measuring the child's height against a machine or against the buttons on his coat.

Over a twelve-year period, Lewis Hine photographed more than five thousand haunting images of working children. Not all children were equally represented in Hine's images. He photographed white children more often than black children, despite the significant numbers of black children who also worked.

Yet the photographs were a start, as people all over the United States saw Hine's work. The pictures said it all: working children were horribly exploited.

By 1909 all but six states had enacted a minimum age for working in factories. By 1914, thirty-five states had minimum age restrictions of fourteen

Children pulled sugar beets and "topped" them, using large sharp knives. Children then carried bushels of the beets, as heavy as twenty to forty pounds, to weighing stations several hundred yards away. Photography Collection, University of Maryland Baltimore County

In canneries, the acid found in many foods was powerful enough to eat the skin on children's fingers. Library of Congress

for workers; eighteen states had an eight-hour day for factory work; thirty-four states prohibited night work for children under age sixteen; thirty-six states provided for factory inspection; and thirty-eight states had minimum educational requirements.

Forty-two states developed a system of work certificates. In order to be granted a work certificate, a child had to provide proof of age and an ability to read and write. In some states, the child also had to pass a physical examination. Truant officers, school authorities, labor officials, constables or sheriffs, or factory inspectors were sent out to check for underage working children.

The state child labor laws did not work as well or as quickly as the reformers had hoped. It took twenty more years for federal child labor laws to be enacted. Children would continue to work long hours for low wages, especially in sweatshops, in fields, and in the southern cotton mills.

In reality, no law could prevent child labor. Kids would work as long as their parents needed the money, employers benefited from cheap labor, and people bought the products that children produced. Enforcement and change would require children, parents, employers, and authorities to work together.

Kids on Strike

Many kids who went on strike found their calling and continued to work for reform throughout their lives.

New England mill girl Harriet Hanson worked for thirteen years and was proud of her honorable discharge at age twenty-three. A year later, she married a young newspaper editor, William Robinson. She became a writer and reformer, fighting for the abolition of slavery and for women's suffrage. In her autobiography, Harriet wrote, "A woman ought to be as proud of being self-made as a man . . . proud enough to assert the fact in her life and in her works."

John Mitchell's childhood experience convinced him that the mine workers needed a union. For John, it wasn't enough simply to be a member of the United Mine Workers. He became their leader and fought tire-

The National Child Labor Committee published Hine's photographs in newspapers, magazines, and pamphlets. The photographs also became part of traveling exhibition panels. Photography Collection, University of Maryland Baltimore County

Pauline Newman was a favorite speaker on women's suffrage and labor.

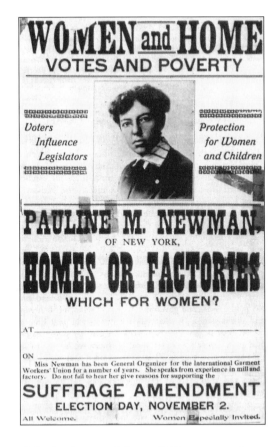

lessly to improve their working and living conditions. For years after he left the anthracite region, his photograph hung in many mine workers' homes.

The rent strike leader Pauline Newman became a Women's Trade Union League activist. She traveled widely, speaking on suffrage. Often she was heckled as she spoke. "Go home, feed the kids," men shouted. She always answered them back, often getting the crowd to side with her. A male colleague later described Pauline as "capable of smoking a cigar with the best of them." For more than seventy years, until she was nearly ninety years old, Pauline organized for the International Ladies' Garment Workers' Union. In her later years, she served as their education director.

"I had fire in my mouth," Clara Lemlich said of her younger days. The tiny, fiery speaker who roused the New York City shirtwaist workers to a general strike in 1909 remained committed to organizing women for the rest of her life. Clara married and had children, but she never stopped building neighborhood coalitions of housewives. Up until her final days in a nursing home, she campaigned for public housing, education, and price controls on food and rent.

Sometimes family members were surprised by the young activists living among them. As a teenager, Agnes Nestor was elected to be spokesperson for her fellow glovemakers. Years later, Agnes reflected on her sister Mary's doubt in her speaking ability. "This seems amusing to me now," said Agnes. "Also to certain of my friends who were present at that meeting, for they assure me I have been talking ever since." It was true: Agnes became vice president of the International Glove Workers Union and president of the Chicago Women's Trade Union League. She spent the rest of her life organizing workers and fighting for reform.

Gus Rangnow, the eleven-year-old boy who accompanied Mother Jones on the march to see President Roosevelt, returned to work. He later served in World War I, then joined the Philadelphia police force. As a police sergeant, Gus was con-

Gus Rangnow was a thirty-seven-year veteran of the Philadelphia police force. He remained concerned about the welfare of children all of his life.
Tom Harrison

cerned about the juvenile crime and gangs that he saw on his beat in North Philadelphia. Wanting to help the kids, he founded the Police Athletic League in 1946. Today, the League continues to bring police and children together, through programs in sports, substance abuse prevention, good citizenship, and career outreach programs.

After the Lawrence children returned home from Washington, D.C., and their temporary homes in the Northeast, they didn't talk much about the strike. Although they had vivid memories, many chose to return to quiet lives, perhaps to protect themselves and their families from reprisals.

Camella Teoli never told her children about her accident, the Lawrence strike, her trip to Washington, or her testimony in front of the House committee. During the last years of her life, Camella lived with her daughter.

Library of Congress

Every day Camella's daughter saw the bald spot as she combed her mother's hair into a bun, but she didn't know what had caused it. After Camella's death, her daughter was given the transcripts of Camella's testimony. "Now I have a past," her daughter said. "Now my son has a history."

They Made a Difference

The history of child labor is the story of millions of kids who worked long, grueling hours for meager wages. It's the story of kids who helped to support their families and who improved their families' lives. It's the story of kids who only wanted what adults wanted: a fair day's work, a fair day's wage, a safe working environment, and better living conditions.

It's also the story of kids who discovered power when they banded together for a common cause. Sometimes they won big—like the New York City newsies and bootblacks. Sometimes they helped their parents and other grown-ups win—like the Pennsylvania anthracite mine workers and the Lawrence, Massachusetts, mill workers. Sometimes they won small—like the Lower East Side tenants and some of the New York City and Philadelphia shirtwaist makers. Often they didn't win at all—like the New York City messenger boys. Or their success wasn't recognized until years later—like the mill children who marched alongside Mother Jones.

No matter what kind of wins they had, the children fought abuses and demanded social justice and human dignity. They developed a common understanding from their shared living and working experiences, even though they didn't share the same language, traditions, or customs. Kids on strike made a difference.

A Timeline of
Federal Child Labor Laws

1916, 1919   First federal child labor laws are passed by Congress and signed by President Woodrow Wilson. The laws establish fourteen as the minimum age for children to work in industries and limit the workday to eight hours for children ages fourteen to sixteen. No protection is given to children who work in street trades or in agriculture.

1918, 1922   Both federal child labor laws are declared unconstitutional: the first in 1918, and the second in 1922. The Supreme Court ruled that the federal government did not have the authority to enact federal laws over state laws.

1924   A child labor amendment to the Constitution is proposed. The amendment would grant Congress the power to "limit, regulate, and prohibit the labor of persons under eighteen years of age." The amendment does not provide for educational standards or physical fitness restrictions. Opponents criticize the amendment, saying that an age limit of sixteen is high enough and that "labor" is not defined. The 1924 Child Labor Amendment is not ratified.

1929–1933   During the Depression, an estimated ten million adults are out of work, but children continue to work in growing numbers in sweatshops, especially in the garment industries. The National Child Labor Committee lobbies to convince legislators that establishing a minimum working age for children will keep children in school and create jobs for adults.

April–May 1933   A series of children's strikes erupt in Pennsylvania shirt factories. Mrs. Gifford Pinchot, wife of the Pennsylvania governor, joins the children's picket lines in Allentown and leads them in a parade. The four hundred strikers, mostly girls between the ages of thirteen and eighteen, earn as little as fifty-seven cents a week for long hours in unpleasant factory surroundings. When a young girl asks Mrs. Pinchot if it's ladylike to picket, Mrs. Pinchot responds: "You are obliged to do it out of the consideration for the many others who are suffering from low wages if not for yourselves. Our ancestors fought their revolution. We must fight our economic revolution."

May 10, 1933   Allentown children win pay increases and a guaranteed minimum wage. More children's strikes erupt in the Philadelphia area and in western Pennsylvania.

1933   Franklin Delano Roosevelt's New Deal creates the National Industrial Recovery Act (NIRA), an attempt to relieve industrial unemployment by increasing wages and by eliminating unfair trade practices. Under NIRA, minimum age standards are incorporated in five hundred separate industrial codes.

1935   The Supreme Court rules that NIRA is unconstitutional because it gives the president too much power. Within a year, the number of employed children increases 150 percent.

1938   The Fair Labor Standards Act (FLSA) is passed. This act prohibits the employment of any child under the age of fourteen and children under sixteen while school is in session. It also restricts children from working on goods shipped across the state lines or sent overseas, and it establishes eighteen as the minimum age to work at trades considered hazardous.

Today a worldwide fight against child labor continues. According to the International Labour Organization, an estimated 250 million girls and boys between the ages of five and fourteen are exploited in sweatshops, farm fields, brothels, and on city streets. Most working children live in developing nations, but hundreds of thousands live in industrialized nations, like the United States.

Bibliography

General Sources

Abbott, Grace. *The Child and the State: Selected Documents.* Chicago: University of Chicago Press, 1938.

Addams, Jane. *Twenty Years at Hull-House.* New York: Macmillan, 1911.

Baxandall, Rosalyn, Linda Gordon, and Susan Reverby, eds. *America's Working Women.* New York: Random House, 1976.

Bremner, Robert, ed. *Children and Youth in America: A Documentary History.* Vol. II. 1860–1932. Cambridge, Mass.: Harvard University Press, 1971.

Clement, Priscilla Ferguson. *Growing Pains: Children in the Industrial Age, 1850–1890.* New York: Twayne, 1997.

Common, John R. *History of Labour in the United States.* Vol. VI. Reprint. New York: Augustus M. Kelley, 1966.

Cunningham, Hugh. *Children and Childhood in Western Society Since 1500.* New York: Longman Publishers, 1995.

Davidson, Elizabeth H. *Child Labor Legislation in the Southern States.* Chapel Hill: University of North Carolina Press, 1939.

Foner, Philip S. *Women and the American Labor Movement: From Colonial Times to the Eve of World War I.* New York: Free Press, 1979.

—— and Ronald L. Lewis, eds. *Black Workers: A Documentary History from Colonial Times to the Present.* Philadelphia: Temple University Press, 1989.

Johnsen, Julia, ed. *Selected Articles on Child Labor.* New York: H. W. Wilson, 1925.

Kingsbury, Susan M., ed. *Labor Laws and Their Enforcement.* New York: Arno Press, 1971.

Lens, Sidney. *The Labor Wars: From the Molly Maguires to the Sitdowns.* New York: Doubleday, 1973.

——. *Strikemakers and Strikebreakers.* New York: Lodestar, 1985.

Lumpkin, Katherine DuPre, and Dorothy Wolff Douglas. *Child Workers in America.* New York: International Publishers, 1937.

McKelway, A. J. *Uniform Child Labor Laws.* 1911. Reprint. New York: Kraus Reprint Co., 1970.

Mofford, Julia, ed. *Child Labor in America.* Carlisle, Mass.: Discovery Enterprises, Ltd., 1997.

National Child Labor Committee. *Child Labor and the Republic.* New York: National Child Labor Committee, 1907.

Ogburn, William F. *Progress and Uniformity in Child-Labor Legislation: A Study in Statistical Measurement.* 1912. Reprint. New York: AMS Press, 1968.

Riis, Jacob. *The Battle with the Slum.* 1902. Reprint. Montclair, N.J.: Patterson Smith, 1969.

——. *Children of the Poor.* 1892. Reprint. New York: Arno Press, 1971.

——. *Children of the Tenements.* New York: Macmillan, 1905.

——. *How the Other Half Lives.* New York: Sagamore Press, 1957.

Roediger, David R., and Philip S. Foner. *Our Own Time: A History of American Labor and the Working Day.* New York: Greenwood Press, 1989.

Spargo, John. *The Bitter Cry of the Children.* 1906. Reprint. Chicago: Quadrangle Books, 1968.

Stein, Leon, ed. *Out of the Sweatshop: The Struggle for Industrial Democracy.* New York: Quadrangle Press/New York Times Book Company, 1977.

Trattner, William I. *Crusade for the Children: A History of the National Child Labor Committee and Child Labor Reform in America.* Chicago: Quadrangle Books, 1970.

Wertheimer, Barbara Mayer. *We Were There: The Story of Working Women in America.* New York: Pantheon Books, 1977.

White House Conference on Child Health and Protection. *Child Labor: Report of the Subcommittee on Child Labor.* New York: Century, 1932.

Chapter Sources

Introduction and Chapter One

Dublin, Thomas. *Transforming Women's Work: New England Lives in the Industrial Revolution.* New York: Cornell University Press, 1994.

——. *Lowell: The Story of an Industrial City.* Official National Park Handbook 140. Division of Publications, National Park Service, Washington, D.C., 1992.

——. *Women at Work: The Transformation of Work and Community in Lowell, Massachusetts.* New York: Columbia University Press, 1979.

Eisler, Benita, ed. *The Lowell Offering: Writings by New England Mill Women (1840–1845).* Philadelphia: J. B. Lippincott Company, 1977.

Gersuny, Carl. "'A Devil in Petticoats' and Just Cause," *Business History Review.* Vol. 50, Summer 1976.

Josephson, Hannah. *The Golden Threads: New England's Mill Girls and Magnates.* New York: Russell and Russell, 1949.

Larcom, Lucy. *A New England Girlhood.* Gloucester, Mass.: Peter Smith, 1973.

New York Evening Post, July 29 and August 1, 5, 8, 1828.

Priddy, Al [Frederick Brown]. *Through the Mill: The Life of a Mill-Boy.* Boston: Pilgrim Press, 1911.

Robinson, Harriet Hanson. *Loom and Spindle, or Life Among the Early Mill Girls.* Kailua, Hawaii: Press Pacifica, 1976.

Weisman, JoAnne B., ed. *The Lowell Mill Girls: Life in the Factory.* Carlisle, Mass.: Discovery Enterprises, 1991.

CHAPTER TWO

Andriole, Frank. Personal Interview, Scranton, Penn., January 8, 1998.

Brooklyn Eagle, July 21, 24, 25, 28, August, 1899.

Churchill, F. S. "The Effect of Irregular Hours Upon the Child's Health," *The Child in the City.* Sophonisba P. Breckinridge, ed. 1912. Reprint. New York: Arno Press, 1970.

Dobbs, John Wesley. *WPA Life History.* Washington, D.C.: Library of Congress, December 2, 1939.

Hoben, Allan. "The City Street," *The Child in the City.* Sophonisba P. Breckinridge, ed. 1912. Reprint. New York: Arno Press, 1970.

Kelley, Florence. "The Street Trader Under Illinois Law," *The Child in the City.* Sophonisba P. Breckinridge, ed. 1912. Reprint. New York: Arno Press, 1970.

Marcus, Philip. *WPA Life History.* Washington, D.C.: Library of Congress, May 18, 1939.

Nasaw, David. *Children of the City At Work and At Play.* New York: Oxford University Press, 1985.

New York Sun, July 22–25, 27, 28, 1899.

New York Times, July 21–31 and August 1, 6, 8, 1899.

Poole, Ernest. "Waifs of the Street," *McClure's Magazine,* May 1903.

Thrasher, Frederick M. Ph.D. *The Gang.* Chicago: University of Chicago Press, 1936.

Zueblin, Charles. "The City Child at Play," *The Child in the City*. Sophonisba P. Breckinridge, ed. 1912. Reprint. New York: Arno Press, 1970.

CHAPTER THREE

Basch, Francoise. "The Shirtwaist Strike in History and Myth" in Theresa S. Malkiel, *The Diary of a Shirtwaist Striker*. 1910. Reprint. New York: Cornell University Press, 1990.

Bernheimer, Charles S. "Rent Strikes and Crowded Neighborhoods," *Outlook*, January 18, 1908.

———. "High Rents on New York's East Side," *Charities and the Commons*. January 18, 1908.

Dreiser, Theodore. *The Color of a Great City*. New York: Boni and Liveright, 1923.

Kelley, Florence. "Efficiency in Factory Inspection," *The Child in the City*. Sophonisba P. Breckinridge, ed. 1912. Reprint. New York: Arno Press, 1970.

Lawson, Ronald. "The Rent Strike in New York City, 1904–1980: The Evolution of a Social Movement Strategy," *Journal of Urban History*. Vol. 10, No. 3, May 1983.

LeMay, Philippe. *WPA Life History*. Washington D.C.: Library of Congress, 1938.

New York Evening Journal, December 26–30, 1907 and January 2, 3, 6, 7, 1908.

New York Herald, December 23–30, 1907 and January 5–7, 9, 1908.

New York Times, December 26–30, 1907 and January 1–9, 27, 1908.

Newman, Pauline. *Letter to Michael and Hugh*. Typescript 6036/008. Ithaca, N.Y.: ILGWU Archives, Kheel Center, Cornell University, May 1951.

———. Oral History, Interview by Barbara Wertheimer, Women's Trade Union League Papers. Chicago: Chicago Historical Society, November 1976.

Orleck, Annelise. *Common Sense and a Little Fire*. Chapel Hill: University of North Carolina Press, 1995.

Rousseau, Victor. "Low Rent or No Rent," *Harpers Weekly*. January 25, 1908.

Schneiderman, Rose. *All for One*. New York: Paul S. Erikson, 1967.

CHAPTER FOUR

"Aftermath." *United Mine Workers' Journal*. November 23, 1897.

Bartoletti, Susan Campbell. *Growing Up in Coal Country*. Boston: Houghton Mifflin, 1996.

Bodnar, John. *Anthracite People: Families, Unions and Work, 1900–1940.* Harrisburg, Pa.: Pennsylvania Historical and Museum Commission, 1983.

Greene, Victor R. *The Slavic Community on Strike: Immigrant Labor in Pennsylvania Anthracite.* Notre Dame, Ind.: University of Notre Dame Press, 1968.

Hazleton Daily Standard, August 12–September 20, 1897.

Miller, Donald L., and Richard E. Sharpless. *The Kingdom of Coal: Work, Enterprise, and Ethnic Communities in the Mine Fields.* Philadelphia: University of Pennsylvania Press, 1985.

Nichols, Francis H. "Children of the Coal Shadow." *Coal Towns: A Contemporary Perspective, 1899–1923.* Edited by Harold Aurand. Lexington, Mass.: Ginn Custom Publishing, 1980.

Norris, Frank. "Life in the Mining Region: A Study in Strike-Time Conditions of Living in Representative Mining Towns," *Everybody's Magazine.* September 7, 1902.

Novak, Michael. *The Guns of Lattimer: The True Story of a Massacre and a Trial, August 1897–March 1898.* New York: Basic Books, 1978.

Pinkowski, Edward. *Lattimer Massacre.* Philadelphia: Sunshine Press, 1950.

Scranton Times, November and December 1902.

Trachtenberg, Alexander. *The History of Legislation for the Protection of Coal Miners in Pennsylvania, 1824–1915.* New York: International Publishers, 1942.

U.S. Anthracite Coal Strike Commission, *Report to the President in the Anthracite Strike of May-October, 1902.* Washington, D.C.: 58 Congress, Special Session, Doc. 6, 1903.

Wilkes-Barre Leader, August 12–September 20, 1897.

Wilkes-Barre Record, August 12–September 20, 1897.

Works Progress Administration, Federal Writers' Project, Job No. 54, Record Group 11, 12, 13, 14. Harrisburg, Pa.: Bureau of Archives and History, Pennsylvania Historical and Museum Commission.

CHAPTER FIVE

Fetherling, Dale. *Mother Jones the Miner's Angel: A Portrait.* Carbondale: Southern Illinois Press, 1975.

Harrison, Tom. Personal Correspondence and Papers. Crete, Nebr., August 3, 1998.

Jones, Mary Harris. *The Autobiography of Mother Jones.* Mary Field Parton, ed. 1925. Reprint. Chicago: Charles H. Kerr, 1990.

———. *The Correspondence of Mother Jones.* Edward M. Steel, ed. Pittsburgh: University of Pittsburgh Press, 1985.

———. *Mother Jones Speaks: Collected Writings and Speeches.* Philip S. Foner, ed. New York: Monad Press, 1983.

———. *The Speeches and Writings of Mother Jones.* Edward M. Steel, ed. Pittsburgh: University of Pittsburgh Press, 1988.

Long, Priscilla. *Mother Jones.* Cambridge, Mass.: Red Sun Press, 1976.

McFarland, C. K. "Crusade for Child Laborers: Mother Jones and the March of the Mill Children." *Pennsylvania History.* July 1971.

New York Herald, July 7–August 6, 1903.

New York Times, July 10–12, 14, 17, 18, 20, 24, 27, 1903.

Philadelphia North American, July 7–31 and August 1–6, 1903.

Seder, Jean. *Voices of Kensington: Vanishing Mills, Vanishing Neighborhoods.* Ardmore, Pa.: Whitmore Company, 1982.

Spargo, John. "Child Slaves of Philadelphia," *Comrade.* Fall 1903.

Trenton Times, July 13–31, 1903.

CHAPTER SIX

Jenson, Joan. "Needlework as Art, Craft, and Livelihood Before 1900," *A Needle, A Bobbin, A Strike: Women Needleworkers in America.* Philadelphia: Temple University Press, 1984.

Nestor, Agnes. *Woman's Labor Leader.* Ill.: Bellevue Books Publishing, 1954.

———. Personal Diary and Papers, Women's Trade Union League Papers. Chicago: Chicago Historical Society.

New York Times, December 1909–March 1910; March–April 1911.

Orleck, Annelise. *Common Sense and a Little Fire.* Chapel Hill: University of North Carolina Press, 1995.

Philadelphia Evening Bulletin, December 1909–March 1910.

Schneiderman, Rose. *All for One.* New York: Paul S. Erikson, 1967.

Stein, Leon. *The Triangle Fire.* Philadelphia: J. B. Lippincott Company, 1962.

CHAPTER SEVEN

Cahn, William. *Lawrence 1912: The Bread and Roses Strike.* 1954. Reprint. New York: Pilgrim Press, 1980.

Cameron, Ardis. *Radicals of the Worst Sort: Laboring Women in Lawrence, Massachusetts, 1860–1912.* Chicago: University of Illinois Press, 1993.

Carstens, C. C. "The Children's Exodus from Lawrence," *The Survey.* Vol. 28. April 6, 1912.

City of Lawrence, Massachusetts. *First Annual Report of the Director of the Department of Public Safety.* Lawrence, Mass.: Rushforth's Critic Press, 1913.

Cole, Donald. *Immigrant City: Lawrence, Massachusetts, 1845–1921.* Chapel Hill: University of North Carolina Press, 1963.

Contarino, Rosario. Oral History, Tape 95. Lawrence, Mass.: Immigrant City Archives, April 29, 1982.

Flynn, Elizabeth Gurley. *The Rebel Girl: An Autobiography, My First Life (1906–1926).* New York: International Publishers, 1955.

House Documents. Vol. 138. 62nd Congress, 2nd Session. December 4, 1911–August 26, 1912. Washington, D.C.: Government Printing Office, 1912.

Lawrence Evening Tribune, January–March 1912.

New York Call, January–March 1912.

New York Times, January–March 1912.

Priddy, Al [Frederick Brown]. "Controlling the Passions of Men," *Outlook.* Vol. 102. October 12, 1912.

Yellen, Samuel. *American Labor Struggles.* New York: Harcourt Brace, 1936.

CHAPTER EIGHT

Commercial Advertiser, August 13, 1898.

Curtis, Verna Posever, and Stanley Mallach. *Photography and Reform: Lewis Hine and the National Child Labor Committee.* Milwaukee: Milwaukee Art Museum, 1984.

Kemp, John R., ed. *Lewis Hine: Photographs of Child Labor in the New South.* Jackson: University Press of Mississippi, 1986.

New York Times, July 2, 1911.

Index